Fodor's Pocket Guides
ROME

Welcome to Rome

With evocative ancient ruins, Renaissance art and Baroque architecture, gurgling fountains, the scent of fresh bread wafting out of bakeries, and the sound of church bells tolling and espresso machines hissing, Rome is a feast for the senses. The Eternal City has been drawing travelers for more than 2,500 years and it's still one of the most alluring cities, not just in Europe, but in the world.

Romans often compare the city to a lasagna because it was built in layers over the course of millennia. The deeper you go, the further back in history you'll be. That's why you'll often see ancient ruins, including the Roman Forum, below the modern street level. It also makes public works projects notoriously slow—start digging and you're all but guaranteed to find something ancient. Romans coexist with the past in their everyday lives, walking and driving around archeological sites, admiring fountains fed by ancient aqueducts, and storing wine in cellars built centuries ago.

The city's glories don't lie exclusively in the past, though, and it can be fascinating to observe the juxtaposition between the ancient and the modern in places like the Ara Pacis, where an altar of peace built for the Emperor Caesar Augustus is now housed in a sleek white building designed by Richard Meier. Or take the Piazza Augusto Imperatore, a site where Augustus built his mausoleum in 28 BC that is now flanked by the opulent Bulgari Hotel, occupying a 1930s rationalist building. Romans live in a continuum of history with pride for what has been and a sense of appreciation for the present—the best of which can be experienced with late-afternoon *aperitivos* on one of Rome's piazzas.

As you plan your upcoming travels to Rome, please reconfirm that places are still open and let us know when we need to make updates by writing to us at corrections @fodors.com.

Contents

1 EXPERIENCE ROME 7
   10 Ultimate Experiences 8
   What's Where 14
   Rome Today 16
   What to Eat and Drink in Rome 18
   What to Buy in Rome 20
   Best Museums in Rome 22
   Rome in Every Season 24
   What to Read and Watch 28

2 TRAVEL SMART 31
   Know Before You Go 32
   Getting Here and Around 34
   Essentials 43
   On the Calendar 51
   Helpful Italian Phrases 54
   Great Itineraries 56

3 ANCIENT ROME 59
   Roman Forum Walking Tour 60
   Neighborhood Snapshot 64

4 THE VATICAN 81
   The Vatican Museums Tour 82
   Neighborhood Snapshot 86

5 PIAZZA NAVONA, CAMPO DE' FIORI, AND THE JEWISH GHETTO 99
   Piazza Navona, Campo de' Fiori, and the Jewish Ghetto Walking Tour 100
   Neighborhood Snapshot 104

6 TREVI AND PIAZZA DI SPAGNA 123
   Trevi and Piazza di Spagna Walking Tour 124
   Neighborhood Snapshot 12

7 VILLA BORGHESE AND ENVIRONS ... 145

Villa Borghese and Environs Walking Tour 146

Neighborhood Snapshot........... 150

8 TRASTEVERE, TESTACCIO, AND ENVIRONS......... 167

Trastevere and Testaccio Walking Tour 168

Neighborhood Snapshot........... 172

INDEX...................... 186

ABOUT OUR WRITERS 192

MAPS

Roman Forum Walking Tour........ 61

Ancient Rome ... 68–69

The Vatican Museums Tour 83

The Vatican.... 92–93

Piazza Navona, Campo de' Fiori, and the Jewish Ghetto Walking Tour...... 101

Piazza Navona, Campo de' Fiori, and the Jewish Ghetto....... 108–109

Trevi and Piazza di Spagna Walking Tour 125

Trevi and Piazza di Spagna.... 130–131

Villa Borghese and Environs Walking Tour...... 147

Villa Borghese and Environs..... 154–155

Trastevere and Testaccio Walking Tour...... 169

Trastevere, Monteverde, Aventino, and Testaccio.... 174–175

Chapter 1

EXPERIENCE ROME

1

10 ULTIMATE EXPERIENCES

Rome offers terrific experiences that should be on every traveler's list. Here are Fodor's top picks for a memorable trip.

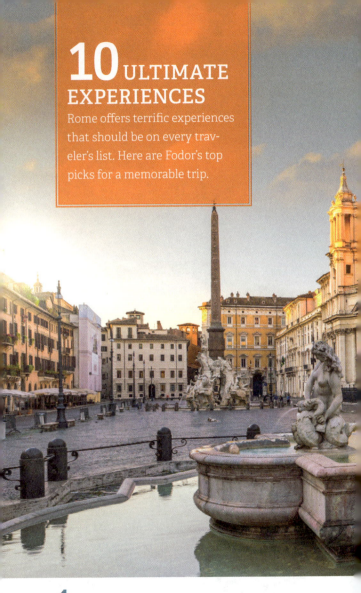

1 Piazza Navona

One of the most popular public spaces in Rome, the magnificent, oval-shaped Piazza Navona is lined with restaurants, gelaterias, souvenir shops, and Baroque art by both Bernini and Borromini. *(Ch. 5)*

2 Aperitivo

After work, Romans love to meet for aperitivo, the Italian happy hour. Any bar worth its salt offers snacks and a selection of cocktails, including the classic Aperol Spritz. *(Ch. 3–8)*

3 The Vatican Museums

As the home base for the Catholic Church and the papacy, the Vatican sees millions of annual visitors, who come to explore its museums and Michelangelo's Sistine Chapel. *(Ch. 4)*

4 Trevi Fountain

One of the few fountains in Rome actually more absorbing than the people crowding around it, the Fontana di Trevi is nothing short of magical. *(Ch. 6)*

5 Galleria Borghese

Only the best could satisfy the aesthetic taste of Cardinal Scipione Borghese, whose artistic holdings within this museum epitomize Baroque Rome. *(Ch. 7)*

6 The Roman Forum

The Forum was a political playground, a center of commerce, and a place where justice was dispensed during the days of the Roman Republic and Empire. *(Ch. 3)*

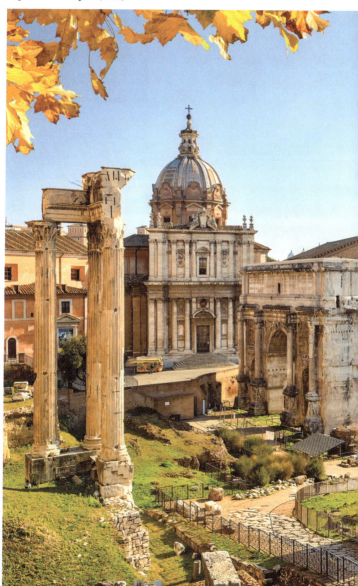

7 La Cucina Romana

Roman specialties tend to be simple, prepared using few ingredients and tried-and-true methods. Classics include fried artichokes, carbonara, and cacio e pepe. *(Ch. 3–8)*

8 Churches

Roman churches, from Santa Maria della Vittoria to San Luigi dei Francesi, are full of impressive art and architecture from Renaissance and Baroque masters. *(Ch. 3–8)*

9 The Colosseum

The most internationally recognized symbol of Rome, this mammoth amphitheater was the site of gladiatorial combats and animal fights. *(Ch. 3)*

10 St. Peter's Basilica

Within the world's most important Catholic church, visit the site of the martyrdom and burial of St. Peter and marvel at Michelangelo's cupola. *(Ch. 4)*

WHAT'S WHERE

1 Ancient Rome. No other archaeological park in the world has so compact a nucleus of fabled sights; nearby Monti has artisan shops, restaurants, bars, and high-end boutiques.

2 The Vatican. An independent sovereign state, the pope's residence draws millions to St. Peter's Basilica and the Vatican Museums. Borgo and Prati are the neighborhoods right outside the Vatican.

3 Piazza Navona, Campo de' Fiori, and the Jewish Ghetto. The Piazza Navona and Campo de' Fiori are busy meeting points, surrounded by restaurants and caffès. The Jewish Ghetto, the historical center of Jewish life in the city, is home to Rome's main synagogue.

4 Trevi and Piazza di Spagna. The Spanish Steps are iconic, and the surrounding area is the place to window-shop, thanks to upscale fashion boutiques. The Trevi Fountain is a short walk away.

5 Villa Borghese and Environs. The Villa Borghese, Rome's vast city park, is home to dazzling museums while nearby Piazza del Popolo is prime people-watching territory.

6 Trastevere, Testaccio, and Environs. These vibrant neighborhoods attract locals and visitors to their restaurants and wine bars. The Janiculum Hill in Trastevere has incomparable views.

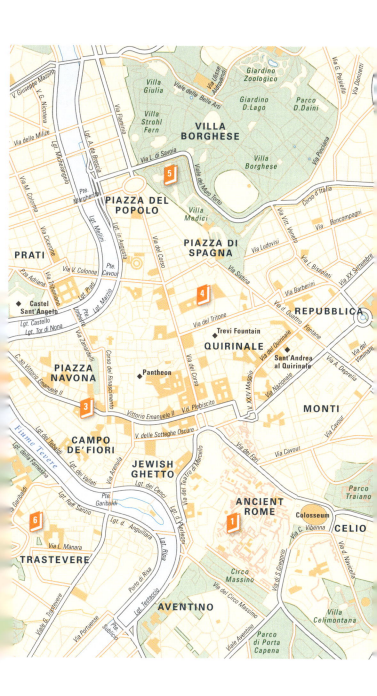

Rome Today

Rome, the Eternal City, is 28 centuries old and yet is still constantly reinventing itself. Here, the glories of ancient times, the pomp of the Renaissance Papacy, and the futuristic architecture of the 20th and 21st centuries all blend miraculously into a harmonious whole. The fact that you can get Wi-Fi in the shadow of 2,000-year-old ruins sort of sums things up, and it's this fusion of old and new and the casual way that Romans live with their weighty history that make this city so unique.

NEW ARCHITECTURE

Rome may be firmly anchored in the distant past, but that's never been an obstacle to its journey into the new millennium. Just look at some of the architectural marvels that have emerged in the last 25 years: the Auditorium Parco della Musica (Renzo Piano, 2002); the Jubilee Church (formerly Chiesa di Dio Padre Misericordioso, Richard Meier, 2003); the Museo dell'Ara Pacis (Richard Meier, 2006); MACRO (Odile Decq, 2010); and the MAXXI (Zaha Hadid, 2010).

In 2011, Rome also built a new bridge—the grandiose Ponte della Musica—over the Tiber River. Looking like two giant white harps rising from the ground, it can be used only by pedestrians and cyclists.

In addition, the Massimiliano Fuksas–designed Roma Convention Center, nicknamed "La Nuvola" for its futuristic suspended cloud shape, opened in 2016.

NEW MODES OF TRANSPORTATION

Romans are anxiously awaiting the completion of the new Metro Linea C, which will cut through the city center at Piazza Venezia and link with both the A and B lines at Ottaviano for St. Peter's and the Colosseum, respectively. Although it is expected to ease surface-traffic congestion considerably, progress on the new line has gone slowly, because every time a shaft is sunk in Roman ground, it reveals some new important archaeological site, and all work halts for the ensuing excavation. Currently, only the peripheral section of Line C is running, connecting with Line A at San Giovanni and continuing eastward to Pigneto and beyond.

More eco-friendly modes of transportation are appearing, too. E-bikes by Uber Jump and electric scooters can be found around the city. You can rent one from Helbiz, Lime by Uber, and Bird via each company's app. Just be careful—riding on the sidewalks is prohibited, and drivers can be rather aggressive.

NEW FOOD TRENDS

Although it's still true that Romans love Roman food, the city's dining scene is becoming (slightly) more international. Rome might never have the diversity of New York or London, but some of its trendiest restaurants and bars serve Mexican tacos and margaritas, sushi, Danish bread and pastries, and even ramen.

You'll also find traditional Roman or Italian restaurants where menus include a few surprising items, like burgers. As puzzling as this tendency might be, it can be nice to have alternatives to the usual trattoria fare.

MORE HOTEL OPTIONS

The pandemic caused a lot of hotel closures, but there's since been a flurry of openings, with lots more to come—and hotels are seriously upping the ante for travelers looking for a fabulous place to stay.

International hospitality companies are investing big in the Eternal City. Some of the new trendy hotels offer unprecedented levels of luxury whereas others offer great style at relatively low price points. Yes, there are classic Marriott and Hilton outposts here, but British brands Hoxton and Soho House, French brand Mama Shelter, and American brands W and EDITION have also arrived on the scene.

In addition, Thai brand Anantara has taken over Palazzo Naiadi on Piazza della Repubblica, and Six Senses has revamped a historic palazzo just off Via del Corso. The Rome-born jewelry brand Bulgari made a splash when it opened a namesake hotel on Piazza Augusto Imperatore. Also watch out for ultra-luxurious openings by Four Seasons and Rosewood.

The influx of new places to stay coupled with pandemic-induced woes means that some older hotels have gone out of business, but others, like the illustrious Hotel de Russie, are gussying up their spaces and revamping their offerings. Overall, it's good news for travelers.

What to Eat and Drink in Rome

SALUMI AND PROSCIUTTO
Romans often start a meal with a meat and cheese board featuring prosciutto, salami, mortadella, and other charcuterie. You can order such meats in restaurants and buy them at stores and delis like the famed Roscioli Salumeria con Cucina, which also has a restaurant in the back.

PIZZA
Rome has two main pizza styles: *pizza tonda* (round pizza) and *pizza al taglio* (by the slice). The typical Roman pizza tonda has a very thin crust and is cooked in a wood-burning oven that reaches extremely hot temperatures; the pizzerie that serve this style tend to open for dinner only. Al taglio pizza has a thicker, focaccia-like crust and is cut into squares; it's sold by weight in places that are generally open all day.

CACIO E PEPE
Meaning "cheese and pepper," this is a simple pasta dish from the *cucina povera*, or rustic cooking, tradition. It's a favorite Roman primo, usually made with *tonnarelli* (fresh egg pasta a bit thicker than spaghetti) and coated with pecorino-cheese sauce and lots of freshly ground black pepper. You can find it at most classic Roman trattorias.

GELATO
For many visitors, their first taste of Italian gelato is revelatory. Its consistency is a cross between regular American ice cream and soft-serve, and the best versions are extremely flavorful and made fresh daily. When choosing a gelateria, avoid the places hawking industrially made gelato in unnatural colors and flavors and opt for the places serving the artisanal stuff.

FRITTI
The classic Roman starter (especially at a pizzeria) is *fritti*, an assortment of fried treats, usually crumbed or in batter. Popular options include *filetti di baccala* (salt cod in batter), *fiori di zucca* (zucchini flowers, usually stuffed with anchovies and mozzarella), and *supplì* (rice balls stuffed with mozzarella and other ingredients).

AMARO COCKTAILS
You can find creations that include *amaro*, the popular bittersweet Italian liqueur, in

most cocktail bars in Rome (it's a main ingredient in drinks like the Aperol Spritz and Negroni). But the best place to sample this Italian staple is Il Marchese, Europe's first amaro bar, where you can choose from around 550 different bottles.

ESPRESSO

Few Romans can live without *il caffè*, so there's no shortage of coffee bars. Real Italian espresso consists of a thimbleful of aromatic black liquid, prepared by a barista in a variety of ways and enjoyed quickly while standing at the bar or leisurely while sitting down (to-go cups are not a thing here).

ARTICHOKES

Winter through spring is artichoke season, and restaurants all over Rome put them on menus as appetizers or side dishes. There are two styles to know: *carciofi alla romana*, i.e., Roman-style artichokes, which are stuffed with garlic and wild Roman mint and cooked in olive oil and water, and *carciofi alla giudia*, Jewish-style artichokes, which are smashed so the leaves open up and then fried to crispy perfection. The former can be found in trattorias all over the city; the place to get the latter is the Jewish Ghetto.

PASTA ALL'AMATRICIANA

The origins of *amatriciana* are in the Lazio town of Amatrice, hence the name. Although it might be made with *bucatini* (spaghetti-like but hollow), *mezze maniche* (short grooved pasta tubes), or rigatoni, this pasta dish always has a tomato-based sauce with *guanciale* (cured pork cheek) and pecorino cheese. You'll find it just about everywhere Roman classics are served.

CODA ALLA VACCINARA

Rome's largest slaughterhouse in the 1800s was in the Testaccio neighborhood, and that's where you'll still find dishes like "oxtail in the style of the cattle butcher." This dish is made from ox or veal tails stewed with tomatoes, carrots,

Espresso

celery, and wine, and usually seasoned with cinnamon. It's simmered for hours and then finished with raisins and pine nuts or bittersweet chocolate.

LA CARBONARA

One of the city's most iconic pasta dishes, carbonara is made with eggs, guanciale, pecorino, and freshly cracked black pepper—never cream. It's sometimes served with spaghetti or rigatoni and is a staple of Roman trattorias.

MARITOZZO

Cornetti (the Italian version of a croissant) are a ubiquitous breakfast staple all over Italy, but if you want to try a true Roman pastry, opt for a *maritozzo*. A soft bun split in half and filled with cream, it's often available at bars and bakeries around the city.

What to Buy in Rome

GOURMET FOOD PRODUCTS
From Roman wine biscuits to locally produced olive oil, vinegar, condiments, and coffee, the city is a great place to stock up on some basics for your kitchen.

LEATHER ITEMS
Italian leather is renowned the world over for its high quality, supple feel, and sturdy craftsmanship. Roman stores that carry leather products abound and range from high fashion designers to boutique shops.

HANDMADE CHOCOLATE
Roman desserts have a unique charm thanks to tasty concoctions like *brutti ma buoni* cookies (which translates to "ugly but good"). But the best tasty treat to bring home is handmade chocolate from an old-school confection shop.

PECORINO ROMANO
Rome's famed sheep's milk cheese, known as pecorino romano, is the star of many classic Roman dishes, from cacio e pepe to carbonara. You can purchase some to take home from multiple delicatessens and cheese shops around town.

LAZIO WINE
Local wineries have been putting the Lazio region on the wine lover's map. Bottles of local wine can be purchased at *enoteche* (wine shops) across the city and even in wine bars and supermarkets.

JEWELRY
Over the years, several delightful boutiques featuring unique handmade jewelry have made their debut in the Eternal City. Don't leave Rome without stepping foot in a specialized *oreficeria*.

Lazio wine

SHOES
From sexy stilettos to strappy sandals to stylish *stivali* (boots), Rome has a *scarpa* (shoe) for every foot. The best place to get your feet wet is in the swanky Piazza di Spagna area, but other (less expensive) boutiques can be found around Piazza Navona and Campo de' Fiori.

DESIGNER CLOTHING
Italians know fashion; that much is indisputable. There are plenty of upscale flagship stores of world-famous brands in Rome, including the likes of Prada, Fendi, and Valentino. But try to browse the city's smaller boutiques, too; you'll be sure to find a piece or two from a lesser-known designer to liven up your wardrobe.

CERAMICS AND DECORATIVE ARTS
Unique pottery, beautiful ceramics, and other decorative arts are at the top of most souvenir shoppers' lists, and Rome is a great place to search for Italian-made items. The best finds are at artisan shops tucked away on winding cobblestone streets.

ANTIQUES AND PRINTS
Rome is one of Italy's happiest hunting grounds for antiques and bric-a-brac. You'll find streets lined with shops groaning under the weight of gilded rococo tables, charming Grand Tour memorabilia, fetching 17th-century engravings of realistic scenes, and many intriguing curios.

Best Museums in Rome

MACRO
The former Peroni brewery in the Repubblica district houses this museum with a focus on Italian art from the 1960s through the present. The building, with its striking red structure, is worth a visit in and of itself.

GALLERIA BORGHESE
It would be hard to find a more beautiful villa filled with a must-see collection of masterpieces by Bernini, Caravaggio, Raphael, Rubens, and Titian. Cardinal Scipione Borghese had the Renaissance villa built in 1612 to display his collection.

MUSEO NAZIONALE ETRUSCO DI VILLA GIULIA
The pre-Roman Etruscans appeared in Italy around 2,000 BC, though no one knows exactly where they originated. To learn more about them, plan a visit to this museum in Villa Giulia, which was built in the mid-1500s.

PALAZZO DORIA PAMPHILJ
For a look at aristocratic Rome, visit this museum in the 15th-century palazzo of the Doria Pamphilj family just south of the Piazza di Spagna. Wander through the Hall of Mirrors—fashioned after the one at Versailles—but don't miss the Old Master paintings.

MUSEI VATICANI
One of the largest museum complexes in the world, the Vatican palaces and museums comprise some 1,400 rooms, galleries, and chapels. By far the most famous attraction is the Sistine Chapel painted by Michelangelo and a team of others, but the Raphael Rooms come in a close second when it comes to must-see works.

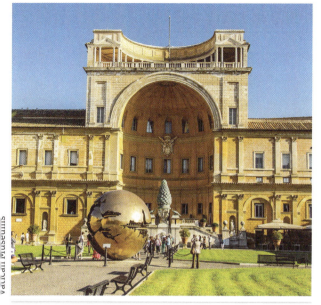

BEST MUSEUMS IN ROME

MUSEI CAPITOLINI
Second in size only to the Vatican Museums, the Capitoline Museums were the world's first public art museums. Two buildings on Michelangelo's Piazza del Campidoglio house a collection spanning from ancient Rome to the Baroque era, with masterpieces that include Caravaggio's *St. John the Baptist*.

GALLERIA NAZIONALE D'ARTE MODERNA E CONTEMPORANEA
A huge, white, Beaux-Arts building in Villa Borghese has one of Italy's most important collections of 19th- and 20th-century art. You'll find works by Degas, Monet, Courbet, Cézanne, and Van Gogh, but there's also an emphasis on Italian Modernism.

MAXXI
Tucked away in the quiet Flaminio neighborhood, the Museo Nazionale delle Arti del XXI Secolo (National Museum of 21st Century Arts)—or MAXXI, for short—proves that there's more to Rome than ancient and Baroque art.

CENTRALE MONTEMARTINI
Nowhere else is the theme of gods and machines more apparent than at this museum. Situated in the Testaccio district, Rome's first power plant now houses the overflow from collections at the Capitoline Museums; the sculptures of men in togas and women in dresses form a poignant contrast to the machinery.

Rome in Every Season

Through April and early May, purple wisteria come to full bloom across Rome.

SPRING

Spring in Rome can be slightly unpredictable, with periods of heavy rain interspersed with sunny days that reach 80 degrees. Usually by late February, there's a whiff of spring in the air, and by April the wisteria are blooming, creating a romantic atmosphere in the city's streets and gardens. The beginning of the season brings vegetables like artichokes, which appear on menus across the city. Next come asparagus, peas, and fava beans, which are transformed into dishes like *vignarola* or may be used to dress pasta.

The biggest holiday on the calendar is Easter, which is celebrated with a festive Sunday lunch that typically includes lamb, chocolate eggs, and *colomba*—a sweet bread—or other sweets. It's immediately followed by *Pasquetta* (Easter Monday), which is a national holiday when Romans head out into the countryside. The next national holidays are the *Festa della Liberazione* (Liberation Day) on April 25 and Labor Day on May 1. Keep an eye out for events like Open House Roma and FAI Spring Days, when many off-limits sites are opened up for visits, tours, and lectures.

The Italian Air Force mounts a demonstration for Festa della Repubblica.

SUMMER

Traditionally considered the high season, summer brings sweltering temperatures, humidity, and crowds. If you're planning a trip in the summer, do as the Romans do: get up and out early, seek refuge from the afternoon heat, resume activities in early evening, and stay up late to enjoy the nighttime breeze. Keep in mind that archeological sites like the Roman Forum have very little shade and few places to sit, so plan your visit to avoid the midday heat. Fortunately, many of Rome's attractions have extended hours in the summer.

Some of the city's ancient monuments, including the Baths of Caracalla and Teatro Marcello, host concerts or performances on summer evenings and there are several music festivals that liven up summer nights. June 2 is the *Festa della Repubblica*, when Italy's unification is celebrated with a parade. The biggest summer holiday, though, is *Ferragosto*, which takes place on August 15. Many shops and restaurants close for anywhere from one to three weeks surrounding Ferragosto, as locals decamp to the seaside. If you don't mind the closures, it can actually be a nice time to be in the city while getting a break from the crowds.

Rome in Every Season

Fall is a beautiful time in Rome, with leaves turning colors across the city.

FALL

Fall is one of the best times of year to visit Rome and Italy in general. September can feel like an extension of summer, but the heat tends to ease in October, bringing warm but comfortable days. Romans have a special term for this time of year—*ottobrata romana*—which they often utter in wistful tones. The month not only brings milder weather but also the traditional harvest time, and there are many festivals in towns within day-tripping distance celebrating seasonal delicacies, including grapes and porcini mushrooms, which also appear as seasonal specials at restaurants around the city.

By November, the tourist crowds generally dissipate, making it a good time to visit—but only if you don't mind slightly cooler temperatures and a little rain. The cultural calendar also comes back in full swing after the summer holidays, with new exhibitions at the city's museums, food festivals, the Rome Film Festival, FAI Autumn Days, and other events. Fall brings fewer public holidays than other seasons. Traditionally, All Saints' Day is celebrated on November 1, but Halloween is becoming popular as well.

The Christmas market arrives in glittering colors to Piazza Navona.

WINTER

Winter is usually mild, with rainy spells and chilly temperatures interspersed with sunny, clear days. The weather may force people indoors, but many restaurants put heat lamps on their terraces or sidewalk seating, so if it's not raining, it's often possible to sit outside even in December and January. The main upside to visiting in the winter is that the low season lasts roughly from November through March, so there are fewer crowds and better rates at hotels. Restaurant reservations are easier to get, too. December is especially festive, as the streets are lit up, Christmas markets pop up in Piazza Navona and Piazza Risorgimento near the Vatican, and hotels deck the halls with elaborate Christmas trees. December 8 is a national holiday celebrating the Immaculate Conception. Many restaurants close on Christmas Eve, Christmas day, and St. Stephen's Day (December 26), but those that stay open often have special holiday menus. New Year's Eve is celebrated with fancy dinners, parties, concerts, and fireworks—the most famous of which may be the concert and fireworks at Circus Maximus. January 6 (Epiphany) is the national holiday that marks the official end of the Christmas season.

What to Read and Watch

LA DOLCE VITA
Just as the names Raphael, Botticelli, Michelangelo, and Da Vinci reign over the Italian art world, filmmakers like Fellini, Rossellini, De Sica, and Antonioni are essential for appreciating Italian (and Roman) cinema. Federico Fellini's classic *La Dolce Vita* follows the busy days and nights of journalist Marcello, taking viewers throughout Rome and its most notable landmarks. Among the film's more artistic and nuanced aspects are gorgeous scenes of nightlife, dining, and general folly in the ancient city's ruin and splendor.

HISTORY OF THE DECLINE AND FALL OF THE ROMAN EMPIRE BY EDWARD GIBBON
Okay, so maybe you do get through all six volumes of this classic text, or maybe they just sit on your bookshelf looking pretty (we're not here to judge). But while there have since been many historical and archaeological discoveries that add to and challenge the conclusions Gibbon made in the late 1700s, this text remains famous and respected for its comprehensive attempt to understand ancient Rome and the causes of its decline. For a more contemporary and abridged source of Roman history, try *SPQR: A History of Ancient Rome* by Mary Beard.

BICYCLE THIEVES
Many Roman films highlight a spirit of unsettling resistance, confusion, and pain during the aftermath of Mussolini's fascist regime—a time that came to define much of contemporary Italy and its art. Vittorio de Sica's neorealist masterpiece captures this atmosphere through the story of a father, son, and one stolen bicycle, taking us through the desperate, dusty streets of Rome after World War II.

THE YOUNG POPE
Although it's unclear how realistic the Vatican politics depicted in this HBO series actually are, this tale about the rise of an unlikely, power-hungry young pope and his ensuing deviance, manipulations, and power-grabs makes for great television. The clever writing and skilled performances (especially by a creepy Jude Law as Pius XIII, the world's first American pope) elevate the show, as does the gorgeous cinematography.

AENEID BY VIRGIL
Because so much of Roman literature (and history) has been built upon the early greats, it's helpful to get some classical poetry under your belt before a trip to Rome. Virgil, Ovid, Horace, or Catullus

(and even Dante or Keats) will do just fine, but the *Aeneid* is arguably the most Roman poem in existence. The long harrowing journey of Aeneas and his soldiers, as they head out of Troy and toward the Italian peninsula, is outlined in this long epic poem, which ends with the early finding (and founding) of Rome, making it a unique literary origin story.

ROMAN HOLIDAY

When all the fascism and papal politics start to get too heavy, turn instead to a light Roman film, the classic *Roman Holiday*. In it, the charms of Gregory Peck and Audrey Hepburn and their whirlwind romance make great vacation fodder, as they ride Vespas through Roman streets, and gallivant through the Piazza del Popolo, around the Colosseum, and other landmarks.

A CLASH OF CIVILIZATIONS OVER AN ELEVATOR IN PIAZZA VITTORIO BY AMARA LAKHOUS

While the plot centers around a murder that takes place in a small apartment building on the Piazza Vittorio, this novel is really about the tenants of said building, a culturally diverse group, whose differences shape the complexity of what it means to be Roman. An author of Algerian descent, Lakhous has a knack for delving into shifting points of view, particularly shining a much needed light on the Muslim immigrant experience in Italy.

LA GRANDE BELLEZZA (THE GREAT BEAUTY)

Paolo Sorrentino's Academy Award–winning film follows an aging writer in contemporary Rome as he examines both his past and present life choices. Moving through the protagonist's partying lifestyle, the film is a modern-day version of *La Dolce Vita* that highlights some of the more lavish, indulgent aspects of Roman life.

THE AGONY AND THE ECSTASY BY IRVING STONE

Reading this 1961 novel provides great context for those who plan to visit the Vatican's most popular artistic sight, the Sistine Chapel. This fictionalized biography of Michelangelo's arduous process details the genius and struggle (along with the politics) that went into his masterful creation. As material for the novel, Stone sourced Michelangelo's original correspondence during the time (almost 500 letters), spent long periods in Rome and Florence, and even worked in a marble quarry and as a sculptor's apprentice.

What to Read and Watch

THE BORGIAS
This historical television drama series gives a fictionalized tale of the very real, very corrupt Borgia family that came from Spain and rose to power and the papacy in Renaissance Italy. Although the show takes historical liberties to build drama, most of the juiciest scandals—torture, bribery, and even incest—are based on real events or longtime rumors about the infamous family.

LOVE AND ANARCHY
Much like her mentor Federico Fellini, Lina Wertmüller—one of Italy's most impressive female directors and the first woman to be nominated for the Best Director Oscar—has a knack for combining humor and folly with political critique and human heartbreak. The film's lovable, blundering star is a countryman determined to murder Mussolini, finding love and friendship in a Roman brothel along the way. This beautiful work is full of Roman sentiment, style, and history, making it a must-see in Italian cinema, as is Wertmüller's slightly darker work, *Seven Beauties*.

GLADIATOR
Russell Crowe takes on ancient Rome as a powerful general who, after a fall from political grace, is taken as a slave and forced to fight as a gladiator in the (digitally re-imagined) Colosseum. The epic film, full of high stakes and high emotions, was a huge box-office hit when it opened in 2000. Although it contains some historical inaccuracies, it's an enjoyable watch for those fascinated by the ins and outs of the political and social structures, power plays, and daily violence of ancient Rome.

EAT, PRAY, LOVE
Elizabeth Gilbert's memoir on what she ate, learned, and loved after leaving a failed marriage to travel the world is divided into three sections and her time spent in Italy, India, and Bali, respectively. The "Eat" portion of Gilbert's journey (the four months she spent in Rome) is perhaps the most enjoyable to read, and provides important travel advice: when in Rome, indulge with abandon. In the movie version, Rome and its feasts are less detailed but more cinematic (and on the plus side, you have Julia Roberts playing Gilbert).

Chapter 2

TRAVEL SMART

Updated by
Laura Itzkowitz

★ **CAPITAL:**
Rome

POPULATION:
4,471,094

LANGUAGE:
Italian

$ CURRENCY:
Euro

COUNTRY CODE:
39

⚠ **EMERGENCIES:**
112

🚗 **DRIVING:**
On the right

⚡ **ELECTRICITY:**
220V/50Hz;
Continental-style
plugs, with two or
three round prongs

⊙ **TIME:**
6 hours ahead of
New York

⊕ **WEB RESOURCES:**
www.turismoroma.it
www.wantedinrome.com
www.italymagazine.com
www.060608.it

Know Before You Go

TAKE ADVANTAGE OF THE ROMA PASS
In addition to single- and multiday transit passes, a three-day Roma Pass (€52) covers unlimited use of buses, trams, and the Metro, plus free admission to two museums or archaeological sites of your choice and discounted entrance to others. A two-day pass is €32 and includes one museum.

NAVIGATING THE CITY IS ACTUALLY PRETTY EASY
Many of Rome's main attractions are concentrated in the *centro storico* (historic center), which encompasses what stood inside the city's 3rd-century walls. The district's borders are roughly the Vatican to the west, Villa Borghese to the north, Termini station to east, and the Colosseum to the south. Although this large area is easier to fully navigate when divided into smaller modern neighborhoods, some main sights are close to one another, making them easy to visit on foot. Rome also has a good network of public transport, both above and below ground.

IT'S HELPFUL TO KNOW HOW TO READ ADDRESSES
In the centro storico, most street names are posted on ceramic-like plaques on the side of buildings, which can make them hard to see. Addresses are fairly straightforward: the street name is followed by the street number, but it's worth noting that Roman street numbering, even in the newer outskirts of town, can be erratic. Usually numbers are even on one side of the street and odd on the other, but sometimes numbers are in ascending consecutive order on one side of the street and descending order on the other side.

BE AWARE OF EXTRA CHARGES
Tourists can be taken advantage of in establishments near major sights, so always check your final bill carefully. It's common to see table service charges or cover charges on menus, but they should be specified. These charges mean tipping is not mandatory, although locals generally round up to the nearest euro of the total amount; at a casual eatery, some coins on the table is good enough. If any surprise fees are on your final bill, don't be afraid to bring this up to the waitstaff. If you're at a bar having coffee, it's customary to leave a coin for your barista. Other charges to be aware of include paying to use the bathroom in some public places and the Tourist City Tax—this is a compulsory per night, per person charge for all hotels, B&Bs, and even Airbnb bookings.

DRESS (AND ACT) APPROPRIATELY WHEN VISITING CHURCHES
If you're planning to visit the Vatican, in particular St. Peter's

Basilica, appropriate clothing and attire must be worn and, at a minimum, shoulders have to be covered. Low-cut or sleeveless tops, miniskirts, and hats are not allowed. Scarves and shawls are available for purchase in and around the Vatican if you turn up unprepared. Modest dress and behavior should also be observed when visiting other religious sites and churches in the city. Do not enter a church while eating or drinking—keep all food items in a bag. Avoid entering altogether when a service is being held. All mobile phones must be on silent.

PRACTICE SOME BASIC ITALIAN ETIQUETTE

Although you may find Rome much more informal than many other European cities, Romans will nevertheless appreciate attempts to abide by local etiquette. When entering an establishment, the key phrases to know are: *buongiorno* (good morning), *buona sera* (good evening), and *salve* (a neutral greeting). When exiting, it's polite to say *grazie* (thank you) or *arrivederci* (goodbye). Italians greet friends with a kiss, usually first on the right cheek, and then on the left. When you meet a new person, shake hands and say *piacere* (pee-ah-*chair*-ay).

BE PREPARED FOR ROMAN TIME

In Italy, almost nothing starts on time except for (sometimes) a theater, opera, or movie showing. Italians even joke about a "15-minute window" before actually being late somewhere. In addition, the day starts a little later than normal here with many shops not opening until 10 am, lunch never happening before 1 pm, and dinner rarely before 8 pm. On Sunday, many independent shops close, and on Monday, most state museums and exhibition halls, plus many restaurants are closed. Pharmacies tend to close for a lunch break and keep night hours (*ora rio notturno*) in rotation.

IT'S USUALLY BEST TO AVOID AUGUST

If you can avoid it, don't travel at all in Italy in mid-August, when much of the population is on the move, especially around Ferragosto, the August 15 national holiday, when cities such as Rome are deserted and many restaurants and shops are closed. If you've done the tourist circuit several times, though, you may enjoy a quieter, emptier version of the city during this time.

THERE ARE WAYS TO AVOID THE CROWDS

While travelers seem to be catching on to what used to be low season in Rome, January, February, and November are still when the city is a little quieter than usual. Advance tickets and private tours that let you skip the ticket lines are highly recommended to ensure hours aren't lost queuing. Spend some time in the less busy neighborhoods like Testaccio and Monti if tourist crowds aren't your thing.

Getting Here and Around

 Air

Flying time to Rome is 7½–8½ hours from New York, 9–10 hours from Chicago, 11–12 hours from Los Angeles, and 2½ hours from London.

AIRPORTS

The principal airport for flights to Rome is Leonardo da Vinci Airport, more commonly known as Fiumicino (FCO). It's 30 km (19 miles) southwest of the city. There is a direct train link with Rome's Termini station on the Leonardo Express train, and there's a local train to Trastevere and Ostiense stations. Rome's other airport is Ciampino (CIA), on Via Appia Nuova, 15 km (9 miles) south of downtown. Ciampino is a national and international hub for many low-cost airlines. There is a train linking Ciampino to Termini station, but you have to take a bus to Ciampino station. There are also a number of shuttle buses running daily.

TRANSFERS BETWEEN FIUMICINO AND DOWNTOWN

If you're driving into the city, follow the signs for Rome and the GRA (the ring road that circles Rome). The direction you take on the GRA depends on where your lodging is located.

If you're staying in the centro storico, follow indications for Roma Centro. Get a map and directions from the car-rental service, and if you aren't using one on your phone, consider renting a GPS as well.

A law implemented by the Comune di Roma requires all Rome taxi drivers to charge a fixed fare of €50 (including four passengers and luggage handling) if your destination is within the Aurelian walls (this covers the centro storico, most of Trastevere, most of the Vatican area, and parts of San Giovanni). If you aren't sure if your hotel falls within the Aurelian walls, ask when you book your room. If your hotel is outside the walls, the cab ride can run you upwards of €60 plus *supplementi* (extra charges) for luggage. (Of course, this also depends on traffic.) The ride from the airport to the city center takes about 30–45 minutes.

Private limousines can be booked at booths in the Arrivals hall; they charge more than taxis but can carry more passengers. The Comune di Roma now has a representative in place outside the International Arrivals hall (Terminal 3), where the taxi stand is located, to help tourists get into a taxi cab. Use only licensed white taxis. When in doubt, always ask for a receipt and write the cab company and taxi's license number down (it's written on a metal plate on the inside of the passenger door). Avoid unauthorized drivers who may approach you in the Arrivals hall; they charge exorbitant, unmetered rates.

Airport Connection charges €22 for one passenger, €28 for two, and minimal fees for each additional passenger. Booking ahead is required. **Airport Shuttle Express** (⊕ *www.airport-shuttleexpress.it*) offers a daily service from/to FCO with stops at all major hotels in the center of Rome. It costs €20 one-way for one passenger, €30 for two, and €10 for each additional passenger. (The rate includes two bags per person.) **Airport Shuttle** provides door-to-door shuttle service, at a cost of €44 for up to three people. Advance booking is recommended.

Two trains link downtown Rome with Fiumicino—a nonstop express and a local. Inquire at the APT tourist information counter in the International Arrivals hall or the train information counter near the tracks to determine which takes you closest to your destination in Rome. The 32-minute nonstop Airport–Termini express (called the **Leonardo Express**) goes directly to Tracks 23 or 24 at Termini station, which is well served by taxis and is a hub of Metro and bus lines. Departures to Termini station run approximately every 15 minutes beginning at 5:38 am from the airport, with a final departure at 11:53 pm. Trains depart Termini station from Tracks 23 and 24 to the airport starting at 4:50 am and the last train leaves at 11:05 pm. Tickets cost €14.

Trenitalia's **FL1,** the commuter rail, leaves from the same tracks and runs to Rome and beyond. The main stops in Rome are at Trastevere (26 minutes), Ostiense (31 minutes), and Tiburtina (48 minutes); at each you can find taxis and public transport connections to other areas of the city. FL1 regional trains run from Fiumicino between 5:57 am and 11:27 pm, with departures every 15 minutes; the schedule is similar going to the airport. Tickets cost €8. For either train, you can buy your ticket at a vending machine, at ticket counters at the airport and at some stations (Termini, Trastevere, Tiburtina), or online at ⊕ *www.trenitalia.com*.

Getting Here and Around

At the airport, stamp the ticket at the gate. At other stations, remember to stamp the ticket in the little yellow or red machine near the track *before* you board. If you fail to stamp your ticket before you board, you could receive a hefty fine, as much as €100 on top of the ticket price. If you book your ticket online, you don't need to print it, but you do need to validate it via a link you'll receive when you book it. You can show the PDF to the ticket controller using your smartphone.

At night, take **COTRAL buses** from the airport to Tiburtina station or Termini station in Rome (50 minutes) and vice versa. Timetables are subject to last-minute changes, so be sure to check before traveling. Tickets either way cost €5 (€7 if purchased on board).

TRANSFERS BETWEEN CIAMPINO AND DOWNTOWN

By car, go north on the Via Appia Nuova into downtown Rome. The taxi fare law implemented by the Comune di Roma that affects Fiumicino applies to this airport, too. All taxi drivers are supposed to charge a fixed fare of €31 (including luggage handling) if your destination is within the Aurelian walls. If your hotel is outside the walls, the cab ride can run you about €60, plus *supplementi* for luggage. The ride takes about 30 minutes. Take only official white cabs with the "taxi" sign on top; unofficial cabs often overcharge disoriented travelers.

Airport Connection Services (⊕ *www.airportconnection.it*) has shuttles that cost €22 for the first passenger and €28 for two. **Airport Shuttle** (⊕ *www.airportshuttle.it*) charges €71.69 for up to three people. The **ATRAL bus** connects Ciampino airport with Termini station via a bus to Ciampino station and then a train. Buses depart from in front of the airport terminal frequently 6:15 am–10:40 pm. The fare is €2.70, and tickets can be bought on the bus. Travel time is approximately 40 minutes.

 Bus

An extensive network of bus lines that covers all of Lazio (the surrounding geographical region of which Rome is the capital) is operated by **COTRAL** (⊕ *www.cotralspa.it*), which stands for Consorzio Trasporti Lazio. There are several main bus stations. Long-distance and suburban COTRAL bus routes terminate either near

Tiburtina station or at outlying Metro stops, such as Rebibbia and Ponte Mammolo (Linea B) and Anagnina (Linea A).

ATAC (⊕ *www.atac.roma.it*), Rome's city transport service, offers reasonable fares for travel in and around Rome, especially with the BIRG (Biglietto Integrale Regionale Giornaliero), which allows you to travel on all the lines (and some railroad lines) up to midnight on the day of the ticket's first validation. The cost of a BIRG depends upon the distance to your destination and how many "zones" you travel through. Because of the extent and complexity of the system, it's a good idea to consult with your hotel concierge, review ATAC's website, or telephone COTRAL's central office when planning a trip.

COTRAL has several buses that leave daily from Rome's Ponte Mammolo (Linea B) Metro station for the town of Tivoli, where Hadrian's Villa and Villa D'Este are located. Flixbuses (⊕ *www.flixbus.it*) leave from Rome's Tiburtina Metro and train station (Linea B) and will take you to Siena and other towns in Tuscany.

While the bus may be an affordable way of moving around, keep in mind that buses can be crowded due to commuter traffic. Just because you've managed to purchase a ticket doesn't mean you're guaranteed a seat. Make sure to arrive early and stand your ground in line. If you are not able to procure a seat, you may be standing for the entire ride.

Car

Driving in Rome isn't recommended, but if you must do so, the main access routes from the north are the A1-E35 (Autostrada del Sole) from Milan and Florence and the A12–E80 highway from Genoa, and the principal route to or from points south, including Naples, is the A1-E45. All highways connect with the Grande Raccordo Anulare Ring Road (GRA), which channels traffic into the city center. Markings on the GRA are confusing: take time to study the route you need. For driving directions, check out ⊕ *www.tuttocitta.it*.

Be extremely mindful of pedestrians and mopeds. Romans are casual jaywalkers who pop out frequently from between parked cars, and scooter drivers weave in and out of traffic.

Getting Here and Around

PARKING

Parking in Rome can be a nightmare. The situation is greatly compounded by the fact that private cars without permits are not allowed access to the centro storico on weekdays 6:30 am–6 pm, Saturday 2 pm–6 pm, or Friday and Saturday nights (11 pm–3 am). Other areas, including Trastevere, Testaccio, and San Lorenzo, are closed to cars at various times. Check the **Roma Mobilità** website for the most up-to-date information. These areas, known as Zona Traffico Limitato (ZTL), are marked by electric signs, and bordering streets have video cameras for photographing license plates. Fines are sent directly to car-rental companies and added to your bill. Check with your hotel regarding appropriate places to park nearby.

Most parking is metered and costs €1–€1.50 per hour (depending on the area) with a limit on total parking time allowed in many places. Spaces with white lines are free; spaces with blue lines are paid; and spaces with yellow lines are for the handicapped only. All other color-coded spaces are reserved for residents or carpooling and require special permits. If you park in one without a permit, your car could be ticketed or towed.

Note that there are parking facilities near the Villa Borghese and the Vatican.

RENTAL CARS

When you reserve a car, ask about cancellation penalties, taxes, drop-off charges (if you're planning to pick the car up in one city and leave it in another), and surcharges (for additional drivers, say, or for driving across regional or country borders or beyond a specific distance from your point of rental). All these things can add substantially to your costs, as can car seats, GPS, and other extras—all of which are best arranged when booking.

Rates in Rome begin at around €40 per day for an economy car with air-conditioning, a manual transmission (note that automatic transmissions are rarer), and unlimited mileage. This includes the 20% Value-Added Tax (VAT, or "IVA" in Italian) on car rentals.

It's usually cheaper to rent a car in advance rather than on arrival. Indeed, booking ahead on a rental company's website can save you as much as €10 per day. There are other reasons to book ahead, though: to ensure availability during busy times of the year or to ensure that you get certain types of cars (automatic transmission, vans, SUVs, exotic sports cars).

In Italy, you must be 21 years of age to rent an economy or subcompact car, and most companies require customers under the age of 23 to pay by credit card. There are no special restrictions on senior-citizen drivers. Upon rental, all companies require credit cards as a warranty; to rent bigger cars (2,000 cc or more), you must often show two credit cards. Debit or check cards are not accepted.

Your own driver's license is acceptable if accompanied by an official translation in Italian. But to be extra safe, an International Driving Permit is a good idea; some rental agencies even require it (ask when booking). It's available from the American or Canadian Automobile Association and, in the United Kingdom, from the Automobile Association or Royal Automobile Club. These international permits are universally recognized, and having one in your wallet may save you a problem with the local authorities.

RULES OF THE ROAD

Driving is on the right, and speed limits are 50 kph (31 mph) in Rome, 110 kph (70 mph) on state and provincial roads, and 130 kph (80 mph) on autostrade, unless otherwise marked. Fines for speeding are uniformly stiff: 10 kph (6 mph) over the speed limit can warrant a fine in the hundreds and even thousands of euros; over 10 kph, and your license could be taken away.

Talking on a mobile phone while driving is strictly prohibited, and if caught, the driver will be issued a fine. Not wearing a seat belt is also against the law. The blood-alcohol content limit for driving is 0.5 gr/l with fines up to €6,000 and the possibility of 12 months imprisonment for surpassing the limit.
■ **TIP→ Note that Italian police have the power to levy on-the-spot fines.**

Whenever the city implements an "Ecological Day" to reduce smog levels, commuters are prohibited from driving their cars during certain hours of the day and in certain areas of the city. These days are usually organized and announced ahead of time, so ask the rental company and/or your hotel if there are any planned.

Ⓜ Public Transport

Although most of Rome's sights are in a relatively circumscribed area, and you can expect to do a lot of walking, the city as a whole is too large to be seen entirely

Getting Here and Around

on foot. Rome's integrated transportation system includes buses and trams (ATAC), the Metropolitana (the subway, or Metro), suburban trains and buses (COTRAL), and the commuter rail run by the state railway (Trenitalia). You can get free city and transit maps at municipal information booths.

Tickets are sold at tobacco shops, newsstands, some coffee bars, automatic ticket machines in Metro stations, some bus stops, and at ATAC ticket booths. You can purchase individual or multiple tickets or a rechargeable contactless card. It's always a good idea to have a few tickets handy so you don't have to hunt for a vendor when you need one.

A ticket (BIT), valid for 100 minutes on any combination of buses and trams and one entrance to the Metro, costs €1.50. A Roma24H ticket, or *biglietto integrato giornaliero* (integrated daily ticket), is valid for 24 hours (from the moment you stamp it) on all public transit and costs €7. You can also purchase a Roma48H (€12.50), a Roma72H (€18), and a CIS (Carta Integrata Settimanale), which is valid for one week (€24). Each option gives unlimited travel on ATAC buses, COTRAL urban bus services, trains for the Lido and Viterbo, and Metro.

If you're going farther afield, or planning to spend more than a week in Rome, think about getting a BIRG (daily regional ticket) or a CIRS (weekly regional ticket) from the railway station. These give you unlimited travel on all state transport throughout the region of Lazio. This can take you as far as the Etruscan city of Tarquinia or medieval Viterbo.

All tickets must be validated by tapping contactless cards or time-stamping tickets in the red or yellow meter boxes aboard buses or in Metro stations immediately prior to boarding. Failure to validate your ticket will result in a fine of €54.90, which you can pay on the ATAC website, in post offices and authorized shops, or by wire transfer. Pay immediately as the fine increases to €104.90 after five days. Some ticket inspectors may be equipped for payment by mobile POS; do not pay the inspectors in cash.

CITY BUS AND TRAM

Although not as fast as the Metro, bus and tram travel within Rome is very scenic and fairly efficient. Note, though, that at peak times, buses can be quite crowded, making walking or taking a taxi a better alternative.

ATAC city buses are red or gray; trams are green. Remember to board at the rear and exit at the middle; some drivers won't let you out the front door, leaving you to scramble through the crowd to exit. Also, don't forget to buy your ticket before boarding and to stamp (validate) it in a machine as soon as you enter. The ticket is good for a transfer and one Metro trip within the next 100 minutes.

Buses and trams run 5:30 am–midnight, after which time there's an extensive network of *notturno* buses (late-night buses) with less-frequent service throughout the city. Be sure the bus you're waiting for is actually running. At bus stops, regular buses are either cited as *feriali,* which means "daily," or don't have any special distinction. Notturno buses have an "N" sign just above the bus number; their schedules are listed beside those for the regular day buses. *Deviata* buses have been rerouted due to road construction or public demonstrations, and *festivi* buses only run on Sunday and holidays; like notturno buses, they have less-frequent service.

The ATAC has a website (⊕ *www.atac.roma.it*) that helps you determine the bus route you need; it even calculates the number of stops and gives you a map directing you to them. To navigate the site, look for the British flag in the upper right-hand corner to change the website into English. Or do as the locals do, and use the Moovit app.

METRO

The Metro (subway), which has three lines, is the easiest and fastest way to get around Rome. There are stops near most main attractions, and street entrances are marked with red "M" signs.

Linea A (red, though indicated in orange on some transit maps) runs from the southeastern part of the city, with stops at San Giovanni in Laterano, Piazza Barberini, Piazza di Spagna, Piazzale Flaminio (Piazza del Popolo), and Ottaviano/San Pietro near the Basilica di San Pietro and Musei Vaticani. **Linea B** (blue), which intersects with Linea A at Termini station, stops near the Colosseum, Circus Maximus, Pyramid (Ostiense station, with trains for Ostia Antica), and Basilica di San Paolo Fuori le Mura. **Linea C** (green) runs from the city's eastern outskirts through Pigneto and meets Linea A at San Giovanni.

Getting Here and Around

The Metro opens at 5:30 am, and the last trains leave the terminus station at either end at 11:30 pm (1:30 am on Friday and Saturday nights). As with buses and trams, it's best to avoid taking the Metro during rush hours, when cars can be extremely crowded. Midmorning and midday through early afternoon tend to be less busy.

🚆 Train

State-owned Trenitalia (⊕ *www.trenitalia.com*) trains are part of the Metrebus system and also serve some destinations that are side trips from Rome. The main Trenitalia stations in Rome are Termini, Tiburtina, Ostiense, and Trastevere. Suburban trains use all of these stations. The Ferrovie COTRAL line departs from a terminal in Piazzale Flaminio, connecting Rome with Viterbo.

Only Trenitalia trains such as Frecciarossa, Frecciargento, and Intercity Plus have first- and second-class compartments. Local trains can be crowded early in the morning and in the evening as many people commute to and from the city, so try to avoid traveling at these times. Plan on arriving early to secure a seat or be ready to stand.

On long-distance routes (to Florence and Venice, for instance), you can either travel by the cheap (but slow) *regionale* trains or the fast, but more expensive, Intercity, Frecciarossa, or Frecciargento, which require seat reservations, available at the station when you buy your ticket, online, or through a travel agent. The state railways' excellent and user-friendly site will help you plan any rail trips in the country. It's best to book ahead to make sure you get the lowest price.

Italy's rails have a private competitor, Italo, whose gorgeous and very fast trains travel between large cities including Naples, Rome, Florence, Bologna, Milan, Venice, and Torino.

Essentials

🍽 Dining

Rome has been known since antiquity for its grand feasts and banquets, and dining out has always been a favorite Roman pastime. Until recently, however, the *buongustaii* (gourmands) often pointed out that the city was distinguished more by its enthusiasm for eating out than for having a multitude of world-class restaurants—but this is changing.

There is a growing slow-food movement—featuring sustainably and locally sourced produce—as well as an increasing focus on catering to diners who want to spend less. The result has been the rise of "street food" restaurants, selling everything from inexpensive, creative takes on the classic *supplì* (Roman fried-rice balls) to sandwiches made using organic ingredients.

Generally speaking, Romans like Roman food, and that's what you'll find in many of the city's trattorias and wine bars. Most chefs prefer freshness over fuss and simplicity of flavor and preparation over complex cooking techniques. Most also stick with the traditional, excelling at dishes that have taken hundreds, sometimes thousands, of years to perfect. Hence, the basic trattoria menu is more or less the same wherever you go, and even the top chefs feature their takes on simple classics like carbonara.

Still, people move to the nation's capital from every corner of the Italian peninsula, so Sicilian, Tuscan, Pugliese, Bolognese, Marchegiano, Sardinian, and northern Italian dishes are all represented. There's also a growing number of restaurants offering good-quality international cuisines—particularly Japanese, Indian, and Ethiopian.

Oddly enough, though, for a nation that prides itself on *la bella figura* ("looking good"), most Romans don't fuss about music, personal space, lighting, or decor. After all, who needs flashy interior design when so much of Roman life takes place outdoors, when dining alfresco in Rome can take place in the middle of a glorious ancient site or a centuries-old piazza?

⇨ *Restaurant reviews throughout this guide have been shortened. For full information, visit Fodors.com. Restaurant prices are the average cost of a main course at dinner or, if dinner is not served, at lunch.*

Essentials

What It Costs in Euros			
$	$$	$$$	$$$$
AT DINNER			
under €15	€15–€24	€25–€35	over €35

RESTAURANT TYPES

There used to be a distinct hierarchy of restaurant types in Rome. A *ristorante* was typically elegant and expensive; a *trattoria* served more traditional, home-style fare in a relaxed atmosphere; and an *osteria* was even more casual, essentially a wine bar and gathering spot that also served food. All these places still exist, but their distinction has blurred considerably. Now, for instance, an osteria in the center of town may be pricier than a ristorante across the street. In addition, *enoteca* is the more contemporary term for a casual wine bar that also serves food.

Although Rome may not boast the grand cafés (here known as *caffè*) of Paris or Vienna, it does have hundreds of small places on pleasant side streets and piazze. The coffee is routinely of high quality. Locals usually stop in for a quickie at the bar, where prices are much lower than for the same drink taken at the table. If you place your order at the counter, ask if you can sit down: some places charge more for table service. Usually you'll pay a cashier first, then give your *scontrino* (receipt) to the person at the counter who fills your order.

HOW TO ORDER: FROM PRIMO TO DOLCE

In a Roman sit-down restaurant, whether a ristorante, trattoria, or osteria, you're expected to order at least two courses. It could be a *primo* (first course, usually pasta, risotto, or soup) followed by a *secondo* (second course, really a "main course" in English parlance, usually meat or fish); an *antipasto* (starter) followed by a primo or secondo; or a primo or secondo and a *dolce* (dessert). Many people consider a full meal to consist of an antipasto, a primo or secondo, and a dolce.

If you're not too hungry, try a pizzeria, where it's common to order just one dish. The handiest places for an afternoon snack are bars, caffès, and pizzerie. For a quick lunch or dinner, head to a *tavola calda,* kind of like a cafeteria where you can order from what's available at the counter and sit and eat at a table.

MEAL TIMES AND RESERVATIONS

Breakfast (*la colazione*) is usually served 7 am–10:30 am, lunch (*il pranzo*) 12:30

pm–2:30 pm, dinner (*la cena*) 7:30 pm–11 pm. Peak times are around 1:30 pm for lunch and 9 pm for dinner. Enoteche are sometimes open in the morning and late afternoon for snacks. Most pizzerie open at 7 or 8 pm and close around midnight or 1 am. Most bars and caffès are open 7 am–8 or 9 pm. Almost all restaurants close one day a week (in most cases Sunday or Monday) and for at least two weeks in August. The city is zoned, however, so that there are always some restaurants in each zone that remain open.

The pace of a sit-down meal may be slower than what you're used to and you won't receive *il conto* (the bill) until you ask for it. Because most Roman restaurants are small and aren't in the business of turning tables, it's best to reserve in advance. Popular restaurants tend to book up days or weeks ahead of time. Even if you walk into a restaurant at 7 pm and see empty tables, the host might not seat you because you likely won't finish your meal before the diners who booked those tables arrive.

 Lodging

Whether you want a simple place to rest your head or a complete cache of exclusive amenities, you have plenty of choices. Indeed, Rome has a wide selection of high-end hotels, bed-and-breakfasts, and designer boutique hotels—options that run the gamut from whimsical to luxurious.

Luxury hotels are justly renowned for sybaritic comforts: fluffy towels, postcard views over Roman rooftops, and silver flatware on white linen atop a groaning breakfast-buffet table. In the more modest categories, however, Rome's hotels don't always meet the standards of space, comfort, quiet, and service found in comparable U.S. properties. Hence, you may find places that have tiny rooms, lumpy beds, and anemic air-conditioning. The good news: if you're flexible, there are happy mediums aplenty.

Location is a good place to start when picking a lodging, and proximity to the main sights is only one consideration. For instance, if a picturesque location is important, stay in one of the small hotels around Piazza Navona or Campo de' Fiori. If luxury is a priority, opt for Piazza di Spagna or beyond the city center, where

Where Should I Stay?

	NEIGHBORHOOD VIBE	PROS	CONS
Around the Vatican: Borgo and Prati	Touristy and not especially atmospheric but has good restaurants and caffès.	Close to the Vatican; pretty quiet at night.	Far from other major attractions and nightlife.
Piazza Navona, Campo de' Fiori, and Jewish Ghetto	Surrounded by most of Rome's major attractions.	Walking distance to good restaurants and shops, as well as museums and monuments.	Convenient but pricey. Lots of hustle and bustle, so street noise can be an issue (the Jewish Ghetto is quieter, though).
Piazza di Spagna	Frequented by high rollers and A-listers.	Has the crème de la crème of Rome's hotels and shops.	Everything is expensive; not very close to central hot spots.
Repubblica	Has a beautiful piazza and is near Termini station without the grungy feel.	Hotels are much cheaper than elsewhere in Rome; convenient to Termini station.	Basic accommodations; the area surrounding Termini station can be iffy.
Villa Borghese and Piazza del Popolo, Monte Mario, and Parioli	Somewhat outside the hubbub and a bit more refined, with fancy boutiques and hotels.	Close to the Piazza di Spagna and shopping; lots of dining options nearby.	Pricey and a bit removed from Piazza Navona and Campo de' Fiori.
Trastevere	Villagelike, with cobblestone alleys, beautiful churches, and mom-and-pop trattorias.	Fun area with great restaurants, bars, and caffès.	Full of students; can be rowdy at night and rambunctious on weekends.
Aventino and Testaccio	Aventino is a relaxing hilltop retreat. Working-class Testaccio is the heart of Rome's nightlife.	Tranquility, amazing views, and spacious rooms await in Aventino. Party in Rome's famous nightlife district, Testaccio.	Transportation difficult on the Aventine Hill; Testaccio is crowded on weekends.
Esquilino	Has some of the more hip and funky neighborhoods in Rome.	Hotels are cheaper than elsewhere in the city; close to Termini station.	Far from main tourist attractions.

quality/price ratios are better, and some hotels have swimming pools.

⇨ *Hotel reviews throughout this guide have been shortened. For full information, visit Fodors.com. Hotel prices are for a standard double room in high season.*

What It Costs in Euros			
$	$$	$$$	$$$$
LODGING FOR TWO			
under €125	€125–€200	€201–€300	over €300

Nightlife

For a great night out, you need only wander as there's entertainment on every corner. Most visitors head to the centro storico; Piazza Navona, Pantheon, Campo de' Fiori, and even Trastevere may be filled with tourists, but they're also beginning to attract niche and boutique bars. (In contrast, the Spanish Steps area is a ghost town by 9 pm.) Monti has lots of bars with alfresco seating and a more local crowd.

Alternatively, you could leave the comfort zone by heading to the Testaccio, San Lorenzo, and Pigneto areas. Indeed, when it comes to clubs and discos, Testaccio is a mecca. Its Via Galvani is Rome's Sunset Strip, where hybrid restaurant-clubs, largely identical in music and crowd, jockey for top ranking. On average, drinks range between €10 and €15, and one is often included with the entrance (€10–€20). In summer, though, many clubs relocate to the beach or the Tiber, so check ahead.

Wherever you go, be sure to follow Rome's rule of thumb: if you see an enoteca, stop in. Though most are tiny and offer a limited antipasti menu, their wine lists are expansive, and they often have a charming gang of regulars. For the linguistically timid, the city also has English and Irish pubs, complete with a steady stream of Guinness; dartboards; and oversize, flat-screen TVs showing rugby and soccer, as well as American football, baseball, and basketball—ideal for those who don't want to miss a playoff game.

Rome offers a cornucopia of evening bacchanalia, from ultra-chic to super-cheap, but most people agree that finding "the scene" requires patience and pursuit. Although word-of-mouth is the best source, entertainment guides like **Romeing** (⊕ *www.romeing.it*) and **2night** (⊕ *2night.it/roma*) have great general information and up-to-date listings of bars and clubs.

Essentials

■ TIP→ **Romans love an after-party, so plenty of nightlife doesn't start until midnight.**

⊕ Health

Throughout Italy, smoking is banned in all public places. This includes trains, buses, and offices, as well as restaurants, pubs, and dance clubs (unless the latter have separate smoking rooms). Fines for breaking the law are exorbitant. Most people skirt it by sitting on open-air terraces. If you're bothered by smoke, sit inside at restaurants, many of which now have air-conditioning.

It's best to travel with your own trusted medications. Should you need medicine while in Italy, though, speak with a physician so you can ensure it is the proper kind and get a prescription for it if necessary. Pharmacies sell aspirin (*l'aspirina*), ibuprofen, acetaminophen, cough syrup, antiseptic creams, and other over-the-counter remedies. Pharmacists are happy to dispense advice and, in the city center especially, almost always speak some English.

⊕ Passports and Visas

All U.S., Canadian, Australian, and New Zealand citizens, even infants, need a valid passport to enter Italy for stays of up to 90 days.

In 2024, Italy and other European Union countries implemented an electronic visa waiver program designed for foreign visitors to the EU from countries that don't require a visa to visit. If you are a citizen of one of the 60 or so non-EU countries that don't require a visa to visit the EU (this includes the United States and the United Kingdom), this means you will now have to "pre-register" your trip through a simple online process that costs €7; this pre-registration covers multiple trips and lasts three years or until your passport expires—whichever comes first. The vast majority of applications should be approved within minutes, but it's still smart to not book flights or hotels until your application is approved. Visit the official ETIAS website at ⊕ *travel-europe.europa.eu/etias_en* to apply. For more helpful information, check out ⊕ *www.etias.com*.

✚ Safety

Rome is like any other major Western city: generally quite safe but with occasional instances of pickpocketing or bag snatching, especially in the busy summer months. Wear your purse, bag, or camera slung across your body bandolier-style, and don't put your belongings on a table or beneath or hanging from a chair at a sidewalk caffè or restaurant.

Pickpockets—who often work in teams—tend to be active wherever tourists gather, including the Roman Forum, Spanish Steps, Piazza Navona, and Piazza di San Pietro. They're also an issue on public transportation, especially buses such as No. 64 (Termini–Stazione di San Pietro); No. 40 Express; and No. 46, which takes you close to St. Peter's Basilica. You should also be wary of pickpockets in transit stations, as well as on subways and trains, especially when making your way through crowded cars.

Women traveling alone will feel safe but should take the same precautions as in any other major Western city. Although Rome doesn't have as big of a gay scene as other European cities, and Italy is still a rather conservative country (gay marriage isn't legal, for instance), LGBTQ+ travelers should, nevertheless, feel welcome and safe here.

🛍 Shopping

DUTY-FREE SHOPPING

Value-Added Tax (VAT, or IVA in Italian) is 22% on clothing and luxury goods, but is already included in the amount on the price tag for consumer goods. All non–EU citizens visiting Italy are entitled to a reimbursement of this tax when purchasing nonperishable goods that total more than €154.95 in a single transaction. If you buy goods in a store that does not participate in the "Tax-Free Italy" program, ask the cashier to issue you a special invoice known as a *fattura,* which must be made out to you and includes the phrase "*Esente IVA ai sensi della legge 38 quarter.*" The bill should indicate the amount of IVA included in the purchase price. Present this invoice and the goods purchased to the Customs Office on your departure from Italy to obtain your tax reimbursement.

ITALIAN SIZES

Unfortunately, Italian sizes are not standard—it is therefore always best to try things on. If you wear a "small," you may be

Essentials

surprised to learn that in Italy, you are a medium. Children's sizes are just as complicated; they are typically based on Italian children's ages. Check labels on all garments, as many are dry clean–only or non–tumble dry. When in doubt about the proper size, ask the shop attendant—most will have an international size chart handy. At open-air markets, where there often isn't any place to try on garments, you'll have to take your best guess: if you're wrong, you may or may not be able to find the vendor the next day to exchange.

Tipping

In Italy, service is almost always included in the menu prices. It's customary to leave an additional 5%–10% tip, or a couple of euros, for the waiter, depending on the quality of service. Tip checkroom attendants €1 per person, restroom attendants €0.50. In both cases tip more in expensive hotels and restaurants. Tip €0.05–€0.10 for whatever you drink standing up at a coffee bar, €0.20–€0.50 or more for table service in a caffè. At a hotel bar, tip €1 and up for a round or two of cocktails, more in the grander hotels.

For tipping taxi drivers, it is acceptable if you round up to the nearest euro, minimum €0.50. Give a barber €1–€1.50 and a hairdresser's assistant €1.50–€4 for a shampoo or cut, depending on the type of establishment and the final bill; 5%–10% is a fair guideline.

On private sightseeing tours, tipping your guides 10% is customary. In museums and other places of interest where admission is free, a contribution is expected; give anything from €0.50 to €1 for one or two people, more if the guardian has been especially helpful. Service station attendants are tipped only for special services. On off-hours there may be station attendants not in uniform working just for tips. Give €0.50 to €1 if they fill up your tank.

In hotels, give the *portiere* (concierge) about 15% of his bill for services, or €2.50–€5 if he has been generally helpful. For two people in a double room, leave the chambermaid about €1 per day, or about €4–€6 a week, in a moderately priced hotel; tip a minimum of €1 for valet or room service. Increase these amounts by one half in an expensive hotel, and double them in a very expensive hotel.

On the Calendar

The City of Eternal Festivals has a bevy of internationally recognized events. In the fall and spring especially, you can see local and international talent in some of Rome's most beautiful venues.

February

Equilibrio. This contemporary dance festival takes place at the Auditorium Parco della Musica, with performances by international choreographers and dancers. ⊕ *www.auditorium.com*.

Street Food Festival. For three days, Eataly's third floor becomes a haven for street food fans. Buy tokens and redeem them for Sicilian *panelle* (chickpea fritters), Tuscan *lampredotto* (tripe sandwiches), *arrosticini* (grilled lamb skewers) from Abruzzo, and more delicacies. Note that although this festival has traditionally been held in February, its scheduling has been in flux in recent years, so check ahead on the timing of it. ⊕ *www.eataly.net*.

March

Green Market Festival. Dedicated to artisan goods and wellness, this relatively new festival features not only craftspeople selling sustainable creations but also a roster of yoga, Tai Chi, Pilates, and mindfulness classes. ⊕ *www.greenmarketfestival.it*.

Spring FAI Days. The Fondo Ambiente Italiano (FAI) produces two series of open days yearly throughout Italy—one in spring and one in fall—during which incredible off-limits treasures of architecture and art are made accessible to the public. Past locations in Rome have included the Casino dell'Aurora Ludovisi, a 16th-century villa with the only ceiling painting attributed to Caravaggio, the prestigious Accademia Nazionale dei Lincei inside Palazzo Corsini (Galileo Galilei was a member), and the 16th-century Palazzo del Collegio Romano, which now houses the Ministry of Culture. ⊕ *fondoambiente.it*.

April

Il Tempietto. This series of unforgettable concerts takes place throughout the year in otherwise inaccessible sites, like the 1st-century Teatro di Marcello. Music runs the gamut from classical to contemporary. ⊕ *www.tempietto.it*.

On the Calendar

June

Estate Romana. Many of the things offered in this summer-long, city-sponsored cultural series are free and take place outdoors along the Tiber River and in piazzas all around the city. Look for cinema events, art programs, theater, book fairs, and guided tours of monuments by night. ⊕ *www.culture.roma.it*.

I Concerti nel Parco. This June-through-August concert series is held in a small park near the Via Appia Antica. Performances start at sunset, last late into the evening, and showcase a variety of musical genres from classical to contemporary. There are some winter events, including Christmas concerts, as well. ⊕ *www.iconcertinelparco.it*.

Pride Week. Much like Pride celebrations across Europe and the U.S., Pride Week in Rome consists of concerts, book and film presentations, and other events—all culminating in a parade. Revelers decked out in drag or swaddled in rainbow flags march from Piazza della Repubblica down Via Merulana toward the Colosseum in an epic celebration of the city's LGBTQ+ community. The parade usually takes place the second Saturday of June. ⊕ *www.romapride.it*.

Rock in Roma. From June through August, various locations throughout Rome, including the massive Ippodromo, host rock's top acts from all over the world. ⊕ *www.rockinroma.com*.

Roma Summer Fest. Past editions of this music festival, which takes place at the Auditorium Parco della Musica from June through August, have included concerts by Elton John, Sting, Leonard Cohen, Bob Dylan, Patti Smith, and Arctic Monkeys. ⊕ *www.auditorium.com*.

Villa Ada Festival. World-class headliners and a beautiful location (in a former monarch's villa) make this one of Europe's most impressive music festivals. ⊕ *www.villaadafestival.it*.

September

RomaEuropa. For six weeks in early fall, this multivenue, avant-garde performing and visual arts program showcases international artists. ⊕ *www.romaeuropa.net.*

October

Festa del Cinema di Roma. Cinephiles head to Rome for two packed weeks of cinema celebration and celebrity spotting. The festival showcases Hollywood hits, Italian indie and experimental films, retrospectives and shorts, and conversations with global cinema icons. ⊕ *www.romacinemafest.it.*

November

Roma Jazz Festival. Throughout the month of November, the Auditorium Parco della Musica is the site of performances by local and international jazz musicians. ⊕ *www.romajazzfestival.it.*

December

Natale Festival. From early December through early January, the Auditorium Parco della Musica hosts a Christmas festival replete with pop, rock, jazz, and gospel concerts as well as ice-skating. ⊕ *www.auditorium.com.*

Vitala Festival. This philanthropic festival, which runs from December through June, presents concerts of soul, rock, and blues at Teatro San Genesio in Prati. ⊕ *www.teatrosangenesio.it.*

Helpful Italian Phrases

BASICS

Yes/no	Sí/No	see/no
Please	Per favore	pear fa-**vo**-ray
Thank you	Grazie	**grah**-tsee-ay
You're welcome	Prego	**pray**-go
I'm sorry (apology)	Mi dispiace	mee dis-pee-**atch**-ay
Excuse me, sorry	Scusi	**skoo**-zee
Good morning/ afternoon	Buongiorno	bwohn-**jor**-no
Good evening	Buona sera	**bwoh**-na **say**-ra
Good-bye	Arrivederci	a-ree-vah-**dare**-chee
Mr. (Sir)	Signore	see-**nyo**-ray
Mrs. (Ma'am)	Signora	see-**nyo**-ra
Miss	Signorina	see-nyo-**ree**-na
Pleased to meet you	Piacere	pee-ah-**chair**-ay

NUMBERS

one-half	mezzo	**mets**-zoh
one	uno	**oo**-no
two	due	**doo**-ay
three	tre	Tray
four	quattro	**kwah**-tro
five	cinque	**cheen**-kway
six	sei	Say
seven	sette	**set**-ay
eight	otto	**oh**-to
nine	nove	**no**-vay
ten	dieci	dee-**eh**-chee
eleven	undici	**oon**-dee-chee
twelve	dodici	**doh**-dee-chee
thirteen	tredici	**trey**-dee-chee
fourteen	quattordici	kwah-**tor**-dee-chee
fifteen	quindici	**kwin**-dee-chee
sixteen	sedici	**say**-dee-chee
seventeen	dicissette	dee-chah-**set**-ay
eighteen	diciotto	dee-chee-**oh**-to
nineteen	diciannove	dee-chee-ahn-**no**-vay
twenty	venti	**vain**-tee
twenty-one	ventuno	**vent**-oo-no
thirty	trenta	**train**-ta
forty	quaranta	kwa-**rahn**-ta
fifty	cinquanta	cheen-**kwahn**-ta
sixty	sessanta	seh-**sahn**-ta
seventy	settanta	seh-**tahn**-ta
eighty	ottanta	o-**tahn**-ta
ninety	novanta	no-**vahn**-ta
one hundred	cento	**chen**-to
one thousand	mille	**mee**-lay
one million	un milione	oon **mill**-oo-nay

USEFUL WORDS AND PHRASES

Do you speak English?	Parla Inglese?	**par**-la een-**glay**-zay
I don't speak Italian	Non parlo italiano	non **par**-lo ee-tal-**yah**-no
I don't understand	Non capisco	non ka-**peess**-ko
I don't know	Non lo so	non lo **so**
I understand	Capisco	ka-**peess**-ko
I'm American	Sono Americano(a)	**so**-no a-may-ree-**kah**-no(a)
I'm British	Sono inglese	so-no een-**glay**-zay
What's your name?	Come si chiama?	**ko**-may see kee-**ah**-ma
My name is ...	Mi chiamo...	mee kee-**ah**-mo
What time is it?	Che ore sono?	kay **o**-ray **so**-no
How?	Come?	**ko**-may
When?	Quando?	**kwan**-doe
Yesterday/ today/ tomorrow	Ieri/oggi/ domani	**yer**-ee/ **o**-jee/ do-**mah**-nee
This morning	Stamattina/ Oggi	sta-ma-**tee**-na/ **o**-jee
Afternoon	Pomeriggio	po-mer-**ee**-jo
Tonight	Stasera	sta-**ser**-a
What?	Che cosa?	kay **ko**-za
What is it?	Che cos'è?	kay ko-**zey**
Why?	Perchè?	pear-**kay**
Who?	Chi?	**Kee**
Where is ...	Dov'è...	doe-**veh**

the train station?	la stazione?	la sta-tsee-**oh**-nay
the subway?	la metropolitana?	la may-tro-po-lee-**tah**-na
the bus stop?	la fermata dell'autobus?	la fer-**mah**-ta del-ow-tor-**booss**
the airport	l'aeroporto	la-er-roh-**por**-toh
the post office?	l'ufficio postale	loo-**fee**-cho po-**stah**-lay
the bank?	la banca?	la **bahn**-ka
the hotel?	l'hotel...?	lo-**tel**
the museum?	Il museo	eel moo-**zay**-o
the hospital?	l'ospedale?	lo-spay-**dah**-lay
the elevator?	l'ascensore	la-shen-**so**-ray
the restrooms?	...il bagno	eel **bahn**-yo
Here/there	Qui/là	kwee/la
Left/right	A sinistra/a destra	a see-**neess**-tra/a **des**-tra
Is it near/far?	È vicino/lontano?	ay vee-**chee**-no/lon-**tah**-no
I'd like ...	Vorrei...	vo-**ray**
a room	una camera	**oo**-na **kah**-may-ra
the key	la chiave	la kee-**ah**-vay
a newspaper	un giornale	oon jore-**nah**-vay
a stamp	un francobollo	oon frahn-ko-**bo**-lo
How much is it?	Quanto costa?	**kwahn**-toe **coast**-a
It's expensive/cheap	È caro/economico	ay **car**-o/ay-ko-**no**-mee-ko
A little/a lot	Poco/tanto	**po**-ko/**tahn**-to
More/less	Più/meno	pee-**oo**/**may**-no
Enough/too (much)	Abbastanza/troppo	a-bas-**tahn**-sa/**tro**-po
I am sick	Sto male	sto **mah**-lay
Call a doctor	Chiama un dottore	kee-**ah**-mah-oondoe-**toe**-ray
Help!	Aiuto!	a-**yoo**-to

DINING OUT

A bottle of ...	Una bottiglia di...	**oo**-na bo-**tee**-lee-ah dee
A cup of ...	Una tazza di...	**oo**-na **tah**-tsa dee
A glass of ...	Un bicchiere di...	oon bee-key-**air**-ay dee
Beer	La birra	la **beer**-rah
Bill/check	Il conto	eel **cone**-toe
Bread	Il pane	eel **pah**-nay
Breakfast	La prima colazione	la **pree**-ma ko-la-**tsee**-oh-nay
Butter	Il burro	eel **boor**-roh
Cocktail/aperitif	L'aperitivo	la-pay-ree-**tee**-vo
Dinner	La cena	la **chen**-a
Fixed-price menu	Menù a prezzo fisso	may-**noo** a **pret**-so **fee**-so
Fork	La forchetta	la for-**ket**-a
I am vegetarian	Sono vegetariano(a)	**so**-no vay-jay-ta-ree-**ah**-no/a
I cannot eat ...	Non posso mangiare	non **pose**-so mahn-gee-**are**-ay
I'd like to order	Vorrei ordinare	vo-**ray** or-dee-**nah**-ray
Is service included?	Il servizio è incluso?	eel ser-**vee**-tzee-o ay een-**kloo**-zo
I'm hungry/thirsty	Ho fame/sede	oh **fah**-meh/**sehd**-ed
It's good/bad	È buono/cattivo	ay **bwo**-bo/ka-**tee**-vo
It's hot/cold	È caldo/freddo	ay **kahl**-doe/**fred**-o
Knife	Il coltello	eel kol-**tel**-o
Lunch	Il pranzo	eel **prahnt**-so
Menu	Il menu	eel may-**noo**
Napkin	Il tovagliolo	eel toe-va-lee-**oh**-lo
Pepper	Il pepe	eel **pep**-peh
Plate	Il piatto	eel pee-**aht**-toe

Great Itineraries

Rome is jam-packed with things to do and see. These are some of our suggested itineraries. Make sure to leave yourself time to just wander and get the feel of the city as well.

ROME IN 1 DAY

Rome wasn't built in a day, but if that's all you have to see it, take a deep breath, strap on some stylish-but-comfy sneakers, and grab a cappuccino to help you get an early start. Get ready for a spectacular sunrise-to-sunset tour of the Ancient City.

Begin near Piazza Navona by getting a coffee at the bar of Sant'Eustachio il Caffè right when it opens at 7:30 am. Close by are two opulently over-the-top monuments that show off Rome at its Baroque best: the church of Sant'Ignazio, with its stunning painted ceiling, and the princely Palazzo Doria Pamphilj, packed with great Old Master paintings. Midmorning, head west a few blocks to find the fabled Pantheon, still looking like Emperor Hadrian might arrive shortly. A few blocks north is San Luigi dei Francesi, home to Caravaggio's earliest major commissions.

Just before lunch, saunter a block or so westward into the gorgeous Piazza Navona, studded with Bernini fountains. Then take Via della Cuccagna (at the piazza's south end) and continue several blocks toward Campo de' Fiori's open-air food market. This is a great place to stop for lunch.

Two more blocks toward the Tiber brings you to one of the most romantic streets of Rome—Via Giulia—laid out by Pope Julius II in the early 16th century. Walk past 10 blocks of Renaissance palazzi and ivy-draped antiques shops to take a bus (from the stop near the Tiber) over to the Vatican.

Gape at St. Peter's Basilica, then hit the treasure-filled Musei Vaticani (for the Sistine Chapel) in the early afternoon. During lunch, the crowds thin out some, but you can avoid lines if you book online at ⊕ *tickets.museivaticani.va* (the €5 service fee is well worth the time saved). Wander for about two hours and then head for the Ottaviano stop near the museum and Metro your way to the Colosseo stop.

Climb up into the Colosseum and picture it full of screaming toga-clad citizens enjoying the spectacle of gladiators in mortal combat. Follow Via dei Fori Imperiali to the entrance of the Roman Forum. Photograph yourself giving a "Friends, Romans, Countrymen" oration (complete with upraised hand) by a crumbling column. At sunset, the Forum closes and the floodlights come on.

March down the Forum's ancient Via Sacra and back out into Via dei Fori Imperiali where you will head around "the wedding cake," the looming Vittorio Emanuele II Monument (Il Vittoriano), to the Campidoglio. Here, on the Capitoline Hill, tour the great ancient Roman art treasures of the Musei Capitolini, and admire the view over the Forum from the Tabularium and toward St. Peter's from the terrace by the museum's caffè. If you're not entering the museum, there is a spectacular view over the Forum from the Capitoline Hill (at the top of Via Monte Tarpeo).

After dinner, hail a cab—or take a long stroll (*passeggiata*) down *La Dolce Vita* memory lane—to the Trevi Fountain, a gorgeous sight at night. Don't forget to toss a coin in over your shoulder to ensure a trip back to Rome.

ROME IN 3 DAYS

More time in Rome will allow you to explore more of the Roman Forum and the Vatican Museums, check out some less touristy sights, and drink your way through hip neighborhoods like Trastevere.

DAY 1: ANCIENT ROME

Spend your first day exploring the likes of the Roman Forum, the Musei Capitolini, and the Colosseum. This area is pretty compact, but you can easily spend a full morning and afternoon exploring its treasures. Try to beat the crowds at the Colosseum by arriving right when it opens at 8:30 am (advance tickets help, too). A guided tour of the Forum is also a good way to make the most out of your afternoon. After your day of sightseeing, stop for a classic Roman dinner in nearby Monti.

DAY 2: THE VATICAN AND PIAZZA NAVONA

Another full day of sightseeing awaits when you make your way to the city-state known as the Vatican. To make the most of your time, book online reservations (for an extra €5) ahead of time, especially if you want a glimpse of the Sistine Chapel. Also, consider booking a tour of the Vatican Museums; most tours last two hours. Be sure to allow time to marvel at St. Peter's Basilica, too. Stop for lunch in nearby Prati, and, when you're done with the Vatican, cross the river and take in the glorious Piazza Navona and its sculptures. Stop by the Pantheon before heading to the area around Campo de' Fiori for dinner at an outdoor

Great Itineraries

restaurant. Afterward, there are plenty of nearby bars to keep you occupied.

DAY 3: PIAZZA DI SPAGNA, VILLA BORGHESE, AND TRASTEVERE

Start your morning with breakfast near the Trevi Fountain. Do some window-shopping along Via Condotti or its surrounding streets as you make your way to the Spanish Steps. Pose for some postcard-worthy photos there before heading to nearby Villa Borghese. If you're sick of museums, feel free to explore Rome's main park and enjoy the great views; if you're up for some more art, the Galleria Borghese is one of the city's best art museums. Afterward, head to trendy Trastevere for dinner, and soak in the cobblestone streets and charming medieval houses as you bar-hop during your last night in town.

IF YOU HAVE MORE TIME

If you have an extra day, head out to Ostica Antica, an ancient port city that is now one of the best preserved archaeological ruins in all of Italy. A train to the site leaves every 15 minutes from the Porta San Paolo station; the trip takes a mere 35 minutes. Take your time exploring these impressive ruins, and be sure to stop for lunch in town, too. Other great day trips include the gorgeous villas in the town of Tivoli, the charming small villages of the Castelli Romani, and the whimsical gardens of Bomarzo.

If you'd rather stay in the city itself, you can take your time exploring churches and cathedrals like Sant'Ignazio or San Clemente. You can also visit gorgeous palaces like the Palazzo Doria Pamphilj, or check out lesser known but impressive museums like the MAXXI or the MACRO. Visiting the ancient Roman road known as the Via Appia Antica and its spooky yet mesmerizing catacombs is another great way to spend an afternoon immersed in Roman history.

Chapter 3

ANCIENT ROME

Updated by
Laura Itzkowitz

Sights	Restaurants	Hotels	Shopping	Nightlife
★★★★★	★★★☆☆	★★☆☆☆	★★☆☆☆	★★☆☆☆

Roman Forum Walking Tour

Looking down at the Roman Forum from the terraces of the Campidoglio allows you to survey two millennia of history in a single glance. Here, in one fabled panorama, are the world's most striking and significant concentrations of historic remains.

1 Start just south of the Forum at ancient Rome's hallmark monument, the Colosseum (with its handy Colosseo Metro stop). Convincingly austere, the Colosseum is the Eternal City's yardstick of history. Take one of the elevators up to level one to glimpse the extensive subterranean passageways that once funneled all the ill-fated animals and gladiators into the arena. Alternatively, see the passageways up close by booking a Full Experience ticket.

2 Leaving the Colosseum behind, admire the Arch of Constantine, standing just to the north of the arena. The largest and best preserved of Rome's triumphal arches, it was erected in AD 315 to celebrate the victory of the emperor Constantine (AD 280–337) over Maxentius. Shortly after this battle, Constantine converted Rome to Christianity.

Walking Tour 101

HIGHLIGHTS
Arches of Septimius Severus, Titus, and Constantine; the Colosseum; the Via Sacra; the Roman Forum.

WHERE TO START
Piazza del Colosseo

LENGTH
2 to 5 hours, depending on your pace and how detailed you wish the visit to be

WHERE TO END
Colonna di Traiano

BEST TIME TO GO
Early morning or late afternoon

WORST TIME TO GO
Midday, when the sun is high and merciless in the Forum, particularly in summer—remember, there are no roofs and few trees to shelter under at these archaeological sites. The Palatine has more shade (and a small air-conditioned museum).

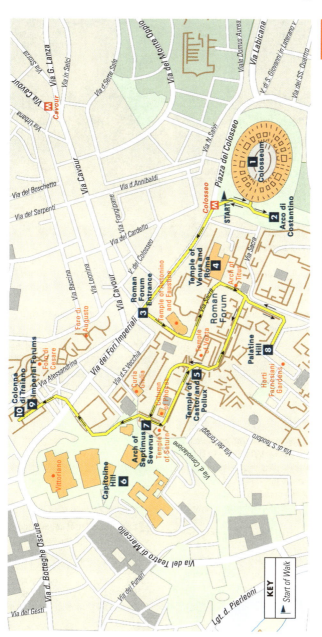

Ancient Rome
ROMAN FORUM WALKING TOUR

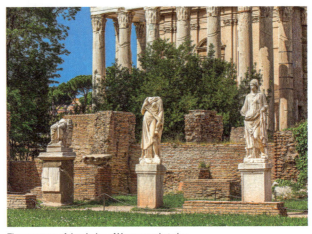

Three statues of the virgins of Vesta remain today.

3 Walk down Via dei Fori Imperiali to the entrance of the Roman Forum, located about halfway down the street from the Colosseum and across from Via Cavour. Immediately upon entering, you'll see the Temple of Antonino and Faustina to your left. It's recognizable thanks to its tall ancient columns that form a portico in front of a church door.

4 From there, you can turn left up the ancient Via Sacra to start at the Forum's southwestern point, where the Temple of Venus and Roma stands. Off to your left, on the spur of hillside jutting from the Palatine Hill, is the famed Arch of Titus. It was erected in AD 81 to celebrate the siege of Jerusalem and is decorated with sculptural reliefs depicting Titus' triumphal parade with soldiers bearing the spoils of war, including a large menorah. Through the arch, photograph the great vista of the entire Forum as it stretches toward Capitoline Hill.

5 Continue your walk toward the Capitoline Hill by strolling over to the Temple of Castor and Pollux, then to the circular Temple of Vesta. In a tradition going back to an age when fire was a precious commodity, the famous vestal virgins kept the fire of Rome burning here. Of the original 20 columns, only three remain, behind which stretch the vast ruins of the House of the Vestal Virgins.

6 Cross the central square and walk back toward the towering Capitoline Hill. You are now entering the midsection of the open area of the Forum proper. To your left, you can see the Column of Phocas.

7 Continue back down the Via Sacra, toward one of the Forum's extant spectaculars, the Arch of Septimius Severus. Continuing left and up the Via Sacra, you reach the base of the celebrated Temple of Saturn.

8 For a better sense of the whole area—a sort of archaeological gestalt—climb onto the Palatine Hill (the stairs are very steep; easier access is up the path by the Arch of Titus) to the terrace at the Horti Farnesiani Gardens for a breathtaking view to put your walking into panoramic context.

9 If you'd rather spare yourself the steep hike up to the Palatine Hill, veer off to the east and visit the Imperial Forums instead. Just past the Curia Giulia there's a path leading to a small bridge that connects the Roman Forum with the Imperial Forums. Walk through an underground passageway and when you emerge, you'll be on the other side of Via dei Fori Imperiali. There you can see the Foro di Augusto and the Foro di Cesare, with the Vittoriano looming just ahead.

10 Continue walking north on the catwalk and you'll soon arrive at the base of the imposing Colonna di Traiano. It was built in AD 113 to celebrate Trajan's victory against the Dacians, featuring battle scenes that served to educate ancient Romans and inspired the Column of Marcus Aurelius in Piazza Colonna.

Colonna di Traiano.

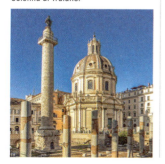

NEIGHBORHOOD SNAPSHOT

TOP EXPERIENCES

- **The Colosseum:** Clamber up the stands above the imperial box and imagine the gory games as Trajan saw them.

- **The Roman Forum:** Walk through crumbling, romantic ruins—a trip back 2,000-plus years—to the heart of one of the greatest empires the world has ever seen.

- **The Campidoglio:** Watch the sun go down over the Forum from the Campidoglio, the best view in town.

- **Capitoline Museums:** See eye-to-eye with the ancients—the busts of emperors and philosophers are more real than ideal.

MAKE THE MOST OF YOUR TIME

This area is relatively compact, but extremely rich in history with plenty to see. Serious history buffs should allow a full day to do the area justice, including an hour in the Colosseum, a few hours in the Forum and on the Palatine Hill, and a couple more hours in the Musei Capitolini. Even for ancient Rome experts, taking a tour can be helpful, but be sure to book a guide in advance.

The longest line in Rome, aside from the one at the Vatican Museums, is at the Colosseum, so book a timed slot online ahead of time (⊕ *www.coopculture.it*). Even with timed entrances, the security line can be long and the interior crowded. From April through October and on weekends year-round, try to book your visit for before 10 am or for an hour or so before closing, when many tour buses have started to depart.

GETTING HERE

- The Colosseo Metro station is right across from the Colosseum and a short walk from both the Roman and Imperial forums, as well as the Palatine Hill. Walking from the heart of the historic center will take about 20 minutes, much of it along the wide Via dei Fori Imperiali. The little electric Bus No. 117 from the center or No. 85 from Termini will also deliver you to the Colosseum's doorstep. Any of the following buses will take you to or near the Roman Forum: Nos. 51, 60, 75, and 87.

Ancient Rome

If you ever wanted to feel like an emperor—with all of ancient Rome (literally) at your feet—head to Michelangelo's famed Piazza del Campidoglio, and make a beeline for the terrace flanking the side of the center building, the Palazzo Senatorio, Rome's ceremonial city hall. The view is breathtaking from this balcony atop the Capitoline Hill.

Spread out before you is the entire Roman Forum, the *caput mundi*—the capital of the known world—for centuries and where many of the world's most important events in the past 2,500 years happened. Here, all Rome shouted as one, "Caesar has been murdered," and crowded to hear Mark Antony's eulogy for the fallen leader. Here, legend has it that St. Paul traversed the Forum en route to his audience with Nero. Here, Roman law and powerful armies were created, keeping the rest of the world at bay for a millennium. And here the Roman emperors staged the biggest blowout extravaganzas ever mounted for the entire population of a city, outdoing even Elizabeth Taylor's entrance in *Cleopatra*.

But after more than 27 centuries of pageantry, you'll find that much has changed in this area. The marble fragments scattered over the Forum area makes all but students of archaeology ask: Is this the grandeur that was Rome? It's not surprising that Shelley and Gibbon once reflected on the adage that *sic transit gloria mundi*—"thus passes the glory of the world." Yet spectacular monuments—the Arch of Septimius Severus, the Palatine Hill, and the Colosseum (looming in the background), among them—remind us that this was, indeed, the birthplace of much of Western civilization.

Before the Christian era, before the emperors, before the powerful republic that ruled the Mediterranean, Rome was founded on seven hills. Two of them, the Capitoline and the Palatine, surround the Roman Forum, where the Romans of the later Republican and imperial ages worshiped deities, debated politics, and wheeled and dealed. It's all history now, but this remains one of the world's most striking and significant concentrations of ancient remains: an emphatic reminder of the genius and power that made Rome the fountainhead of the Western world.

Outside the actual ancient sites, you'll find neighborhoods like Monti and Celio, which are just as much part of Rome's history as its ruins. These are the city's oldest neighborhoods, and today are a charming mix of past and present. Once you're done exploring ancient Rome, these are the easiest places to head for a bite to eat or some shopping.

 Sights

★ **Arco di Settimio Severo** (*Arch of Septimius Severus*)
RUINS | One of the grandest triumphal arches erected by a Roman emperor, this richly decorated monument was built in AD 203 to celebrate Severus's victory over the Parthians. It was once topped by a bronze

Entry Tickets

Admission to many of the sights in Ancient Rome is via a combined ticket that you should purchase in advance online at ⊕ *coopculture.it*. (There's a ticket office at Largo della Salaria Vecchia, but tickets often sell out days or weeks in advance.) The basic combo ticket costs €16 and is good for one entrance to the Roman Forum and the Palatine Hill—which are part of a single continuous complex and include some Imperial Forums sights—and a single, timed-admission entry to the Colosseum. This ticket must be used within 24 hours. The "Full Experience" ticket is good for two consecutive days, costs €22, and allows access to additional attractions.

statuary group depicting a chariot drawn by four (or perhaps as many as six) life-size horses. Masterpieces of Roman statuary, the stone reliefs on the arch were probably based on huge painted panels depicting the event, a kind of visual report on his foreign campaigns that would have been displayed during the emperor's triumphal parade in Rome to impress his subjects (and, like much statuary then, were originally painted in florid, lifelike colors).
✉ *West end of Foro Romano, Monti* ⊕ *www.coopculture.it* 🎟 *€16 24-hr ticket required* Ⓜ *Colosseo*.

★ **Casa di Augustus** (*House of Augustus*)
RUINS | First discovered in the 1970s and only open to the public since 2006, this was the residence of Octavian Augustus (27 BC–AD 14) after his victory at Actium. (Archaeologists have recently found two courtyards rather than one, though, in the style of

The "Bel Air" of ancient Rome, the Palatine Hill was the address of choice for Cicero and Agrippa, as well as the emperors Tiberius, Caligula, and Domitian.

Rome's ancient Greek kings, suggesting Augustus maintained this house after his ascension to prominence.) Four rooms have exquisite examples of decorative frescoes on the walls; startlingly vivid and detailed are the depictions of a narrow stage with side doors, as well as some striking comic theater masks. An exquisitely painted upper room has been identified as the Emperor's study. ✉ *Northwest crest of Palatine Hill, Monti* ⊕ *www.coopculture.it* 🎫 *€22 2-day Full Experience ticket required* Ⓜ *Colosseo.*

Circo Massimo (Circus Maximus)

RUINS | From the belvedere of the Domus Flavia on the Palatine Hill, you can see the Circus Maximus; there's also a great free view from Piazzale Ugo La Malfa on the Aventine Hill side. The giant space where 300,000 spectators once watched chariot races while the emperor looked on is ancient Rome's oldest and largest racetrack; it lies in a natural hollow between the two hills. The oval course stretches about 650 yards from end to end; on certain occasions, there were as many as 24 chariot races a day, and competitions could last for 15 days. The charioteers could amass fortunes rather like the sports stars of today. (The Portuguese Diocles is said to have totted up winnings of 35 million sestertii.)

The noise and the excitement of the crowd must have reached astonishing levels as the charioteers competed in teams, each with their own colors—the Reds, the Blues, etc. Betting also provided Rome's majority of unemployed with a potentially lucrative occupation. The central ridge was the site of two Egyptian

obelisks (now in Piazza del Popolo and Piazza San Giovanni in Laterano). Picture the great chariot race scene from MGM's *Ben-Hur*, and you have an inkling of what this was like. ✉ *Between Palatine and Aventine Hills, Aventino* ☎ *06/0608* 🎟 *€5* Ⓜ *Circo Massimo*.

Colonna di Traiano (*Trajan's Column*)
RUINS | The remarkable series of reliefs spiraling up this column, which has stood in this spot since AD 113, celebrate the emperor's victories over the Dacians in today's Romania. The scenes on the column are an important primary source for information on the Roman army and its tactics. An inscription on the base declares that the column was erected in Trajan's honor and that its height corresponds to the height of the hill that was razed to create a level area for the grandiose Foro di Traiano. The emperor's ashes, no longer here, were kept in a golden urn in a chamber at the column's base; his statue stood atop the column until 1587, when the pope had it replaced with a statue of St. Peter. ✉ *Via del Foro di Traiano, Monti* Ⓜ *Cavour*.

★ Colosseum (*Colosseo*)
RUINS | The most spectacular extant edifice of ancient Rome, the Colosseum has a history that is half gore, half glory. Once able to house 50,000 spectators, it was built to impress Romans with its spectacles involving wild animals and fearsome gladiators from the farthest reaches of the empire. Senators had marble seats up front, the vestal virgins took the ringside position, the plebs sat in wooden tiers at the back, and the masses watched from the top tier. Looming over all was the amazing velarium, an ingenious system of sail-like awnings rigged on ropes and maneuvered by sailors from the imperial fleet, who would unfurl them to protect the arena's occupants from sun or rain.

From the second floor, you can get a bird's-eye view of the hypogeum—the subterranean passageways that were the architectural engine rooms that made the slaughter above proceed like clockwork. In a scene prefiguring something from Dante's *Inferno*, hundreds of beasts would wait to be launched via a series of slave-powered hoists and lifts into the bloodthirsty sand of the arena above.

Designed by order of the emperor Vespasian in AD 72, and completed by his son Titus in AD 80, the arena has a circumference of 573 yards, and its external walls were built with travertine from nearby Tivoli. Its construction was a remarkable feat of engineering, for it stands on marshy terrain reclaimed by draining an artificial lake that formed part of the vast palace of Nero. Originally known as the Flavian amphitheater (Vespasian's and Titus's family name was Flavius), it came to be known as the Colosseum thanks to a colossal gilded bronze statue which once stood nearby.

The legend made famous by the Venerable Bede says that as long as the Colosseum stands, Rome will stand; and when Rome falls, so will the world ... not that the prophecy deterred medieval and Renaissance princes and popes from using the Colosseum as a quarry. In the 19th century, poets came to view the arena by moonlight; today, mellow golden spotlights make the arena a spectacular sight at night, and evening visits are possible with guided tours from May through October.

■ **TIP→ To enter, book a combination ticket (with the Roman Forum and Palatine Hill) in advance online, though if you have a Roma Pass, you can use it.**

Tickets cost €16 plus a €2 online booking surcharge. Aim for early or late slots to minimize lines, as even the preferential lanes get busy in the middle of the day. Alternatively, you can book a tour online with a company (do your research to make sure it's reputable) that lets you skip the line. Avoid the tours sold on the spot around the Colosseum; although you can skip the lines, the tour guides tend to be dry, the tour groups huge, and the tour itself rushed. To see the arena or the underground, you must purchase a special timed-entry ticket with those features, though the arena is included if you buy the Roman Forum–Palatine complex €22 two-day Full Experience ticket. ✉ *Piazza del Colosseo, Colosseo* ☎ *06/39967700* ⊕ *www.coopculture.it* ✉ *Requires either the €16 24-hr ticket or the €22 Full Experience ticket (can include the arena for no additional fee, but it must be specified during the purchase)* Ⓜ *Colosseo*.

★ Musei Capitolini

ART MUSEUM | Surpassed in size and richness only by the Musei Vaticani, the world's first public museum—with the greatest hits of Roman art through the ages, from the ancients to the Baroque—is housed in the Palazzo dei Conservatori and the Palazzo Nuovo, which mirror one another across Michelangelo's famous piazza. The collection was begun by Pope Sixtus IV (the man who built the Sistine Chapel) in 1473, when he donated a room of ancient statuary to the people of the city. This core of the collection includes the She Wolf, which is the symbol of Rome, and the piercing gaze of the Capitoline Brutus.

Buy your ticket and enter the Palazzo dei Conservatori where, in the first courtyard, you'll see the giant head, foot, elbow, and imperially raised finger of the fabled seated statue of Constantine, which once dominated the Basilica of Maxentius in the Forum. Upstairs is the resplendent Sala degli Orazi e Curiazi (Hall of the Horatii and Curatii), decorated with a magnificent gilt ceiling, carved wooden doors, and 16th-century frescoes depicting the history of Rome's legendary origins. At each end of the hall are statues of two of the most important popes of the Baroque era, Urban VIII and Innocent X.

The heart of the museum is the modern Exedra of Marcus Aurelius (Esedra di Marco Aurelio), which displays the spectacular original bronze statue of the Roman emperor whose copy dominates the piazza outside. To the right, the room segues into the area of the Temple of Jupiter, with the ruins of part of its vast base rising organically into the museum space. A reconstruction of the temple and the Capitoline Hill from the Bronze Age to the present day makes for a fascinating glimpse through the ages. On the top floor, the museum's *pinacoteca,* or painting gallery, has some noted Baroque masterpieces, including Caravaggio's *The Fortune Teller* and *St. John the Baptist.*

To get to the Palazzo Nuovo section of the museum, take the stairs or elevator to the basement of the Palazzo dei Conservatori, where the corridor uniting the two contains the Epigraphic Collection, a poignant assembly of ancient gravestones. Just over halfway along the corridor, and before going up into the Palazzo Nuovo, be sure to take the staircase to the right to the Tabularium gallery and its unparalleled view over the Forum.

On the stairs inside the Palazzo Nuovo, you'll be immediately dwarfed by Mars in full military rig and lion-topped sandals. Upstairs is the noted Sala degli Imperatori, lined with busts of Roman emperors, and the Sala dei Filosofi, where busts of philosophers sit in judgment—a fascinating who's who of the ancient world. Within these serried ranks are 48 Roman emperors, ranging from Augustus to Theodosius. Nearby are rooms filled with sculptural masterpieces, including the famed *Dying Gaul,* the *Red Faun* from Hadrian's Villa, and a *Cupid and Psyche.* ✉ *Piazza del Campidoglio, 1, Piazza Venezia* ☏ *06/0608* ⊕ *www.museicapitolini.org* 💶 *€11.50 (€16 with exhibitions); €13.50 with access to Centrale Montemartini; €7 audio guide* Ⓜ *Colosseo.*

★ San Pietro in Vincoli
CHURCH | Michelangelo's *Moses,* carved in the early 16th century for the never-completed tomb of Pope Julius II, has put this church on the map. The tomb was to include dozens of statues

and stand nearly 40 feet tall when installed in St. Peter's Basilica. But only three statues—*Moses* and the two that flank it here, *Leah* and *Rachel*—had been completed when Julius died. Julius's successor as pope, from the rival Medici family, had other plans for Michelangelo, and the tomb was abandoned unfinished.

The fierce power of this remarkable sculpture dominates its setting. People say that you can see the sculptor's profile in the lock of Moses's beard right under his lip and that the pope's profile can also be seen. As for the rest of the church, St. Peter takes second billing to Moses. The reputed sets of chains (*vincoli*) that bound St. Peter during his imprisonment by the Romans in both Jerusalem and Rome are in a bronze and crystal urn under the main altar. Other treasures include a 7th-century mosaic of St. Sebastian, in front of the second altar to the left of the main altar, and, by the door, the tomb of the Pollaiuolo brothers, two 15th-century Florentine artists. ✉ *Piazza di San Pietro in Vincoli, Monti* ☎ *06/97844952* Ⓜ *Cavour*.

★ Santa Maria Maggiore

CHURCH | Despite its florid 18th-century facade, Santa Maria Maggiore is one of the city's oldest churches, built around 440 by Pope Sixtus III. One of Rome's four great pilgrimage churches, it's also the city center's best example of an early Christian basilica—one of the immense, hall-like structures derived from ancient Roman civic buildings and divided into thirds by two great rows of columns marching up the nave. The other three major basilicas in Rome (San Giovanni in Laterano, St. Peter's, and St. Paul Outside the Walls) have been largely rebuilt. Paradoxically, the major reason why this church is such a striking example of early Christian design is that the same man who built the undulating exteriors circa 1740, Ferdinando Fuga, also conscientiously restored the interior, throwing out later additions and, crucially, replacing a number of the great columns.

Precious 5th-century mosaics high on the nave walls and on the triumphal arch in front of the main altar bear splendid testimony to the basilica's venerable age. Those along the nave show 36 scenes from the Old Testament (unfortunately, tough to see clearly without binoculars), and those on the arch illustrate the Annunciation and the Youth of Christ. The resplendent carved-wood ceiling dates from the early 16th century; it's supposed to have been gilded with the first gold brought from the New World. The inlaid marble pavement (called cosmatesque, after the family of master artisans who developed the technique) in the central nave is even older, dating from the 12th century.

The Cappella Sistina (Sistine Chapel), in the right-hand transept, was created by architect Domenico Fontana for Pope Sixtus V in 1585. Elaborately decorated with precious marbles "liberated" from the monuments of ancient Rome, the chapel includes a lower-level museum in which some 13th-century sculptures by Arnolfo da Cambio are all that's left of what was the once richly endowed chapel of the *presepio* (Christmas crèche), looted during the Sack of Rome in 1527.

Directly opposite, on the church's other side, stands the Cappella Paolina (Pauline Chapel), a rich Baroque setting for the tombs of the Borghese popes Paul V—who commissioned the chapel in 1611 with the declared intention of outdoing Sixtus's chapel across the nave—and Clement VIII. The Cappella Sforza (Sforza Chapel) next door was designed by Michelangelo and completed by Della Porta. Just right of the altar, next to his father, lies Gian Lorenzo Bernini; his monument is an engraved slab, as humble as the tombs of his patrons are grand. Above the loggia, the outside mosaic of Christ raising his hand in blessing is one of Rome's most beautiful sights, especially when lighted at night. ✉ *Piazza di Santa Maria Maggiore, Monti* ☎ *06/69886800* Ⓜ *Termini.*

Via Sacra
RUINS | The celebrated "Sacred Way," paved with local volcanic rock, runs through the Roman Forum, lined with temples and shrines. It was also the traditional route of religious and triumphal processions. Pick your way across the paving stones, some rutted with the ironclad wheels of Roman wagons, to walk in the footsteps of Julius Caesar and Marc Antony. ✉ *Monti* ⊕ *www.coopculture.it* 🎟 *€16 24-hr ticket required* Ⓜ *Colosseo.*

🍽 Restaurants

★ Contrario Vineria con Cucina
$$ | **MODERN ITALIAN** | Wine bottles cover just about every inch of wall space in this intimate restaurant a few blocks from the Colosseum, which, perhaps unsurprisingly, also has an encyclopedic wine list. The friendly staff will happily help you navigate the options and suggest pairings for the dishes, which are rooted in tradition but often with a little twist, like the addition of artichokes in their version of *la gricia* (pasta with guanciale and pecorino romano). **Known for:** extensive wine list; slightly revisited versions of traditional dishes; welcoming, helpful staff. 💲 *Average main: €24* ✉ *Via Ostilia, 22, Celio* ☎ *06/7090606* ⊕ *www.ristorantecontrario.com* ⊘ *Closed Sun.* Ⓜ *Colosseo.*

Did You Know?

Hollywood got it wrong, historians got it right: plenty of gladiators died in the Colosseum, pictured here, but early Christians only met their tragic fate in the nearby Circus Maximus arena.

Il Bocconcino
$$ | ROMAN | This charming osteria with burgundy leather booths and vintage advertisements serves forgotten recipes from Rome and Lazio in addition to classic dishes like carbonara and an excellent cacio e pepe with homemade tonnarelli. Don't expect artichokes in July or eggplant in December—the cuisine is strictly seasonal and made using the finest local ingredients. **Known for:** forgotten Roman dishes; cozy interiors; good selection of local wines. $ *Average main: €18* ⌧ *Via Ostilia, 23, Celio* ☎ *06/77079175* ⊕ *www.ilbocconcino.com* ⊗ *Closed Wed.* Ⓜ *Colosseo.*

Il Tempio di Iside
$$$ | SEAFOOD | In an unassuming location between the Colosseum and Piazza San Giovanni, this elegant restaurant with exposed brick arches and white tablecloths serves some of the freshest seafood in the city—with tanks full of live lobsters and crabs to prove it. Owner Francesco Tripodi personally goes to the fish auctions in Fiumicino everyday and presides over the dining room, charismatically dispensing suggestions and taking orders. **Known for:** vast selection of raw appetizers; shrimp catalana; charismatic owner. $ *Average main: €28* ⌧ *Via Pietro Verri, 1, Celio* ☎ *06/77204025* ⊕ *www.isideristorante.it* ⊗ *Closed Sun.* Ⓜ *Manzoni.*

La Taverna dei Fori Imperiali
$$ | ROMAN | Tucked on a cobblestone street at the edge of Monti, this cozy little family-run restaurant is one of the best places to eat near the Forum. An eclectic collection of sketches, photos, and paintings decorates the walls, and the menu offers traditional Roman trattoria fare as well as some creative twists on the classics, like cacio e pepe, usually a simple dish of pasta in a peppery cheese sauce but here featuring black truffle, and burrata-stuffed ravioli. **Known for:** la gricia pasta with seasonal fruit; cozy space with brick arches; friendly servers. $ *Average main: €18* ⌧ *Via della Madonna dei Monti, 9, Monti* ☎ *06/6798643* ⊕ *www.latavernadeiforiimperiali.com* ⊗ *Closed Tues.* Ⓜ *Cavour.*

Rocco Ristorante
$$ | ROMAN | FAMILY | This slightly vintage, slightly trendy trattoria has a timeless quality, with terrazzo floors, vaulted brick ceilings, white tablecloths, vintage photos, sketches, and a Pink Floyd poster lending the place a hip yet easygoing vibe that attracts people of all ages. Or maybe it's the owner, a real Roman character who presides over the dining room, coming to your table and reciting the menu—written on a chalkboard—in case you can't read

it. **Known for:** Italian comfort food; cool, welcoming atmosphere; local favorite spot. ⓢ *Average main: €18* ✉ *Via Giovanni Lanza, 93, Monti* ☎ *06/4870942* ⊕ *www.instagram.com/roccoristorante* ⊘ *Closed Sun. No dinner Sat.* Ⓜ *Vittorio Emanuele, Cavour.*

ViVi Piazza Venezia

$$ | **BISTRO** | For an alternative to the heavy pastas typically found in Roman restaurants, this cheerful bistro inside Palazzo Bonaparte is a great choice. There are plenty of healthy options like excellent salads and poké bowls, as well as heartier fare such as burgers and, yes, pasta. **Known for:** fresh, healthy food; vegan and gluten-free desserts; shabby-chic design. ⓢ *Average main: €15* ✉ *Piazza Venezia, 5, Piazza Venezia* ☎ *06/69228769* ⊕ *www.vivi.it* Ⓜ *Colosseo.*

☕ Coffee and Quick Bites

★ Fatamorgana Monti

$ | **ICE CREAM** | **FAMILY** | The emphasis is on all-natural ingredients at this woman-owned gelateria, which has several locations in Rome, including one near Campo de' Fiori and another in Trastevere. Flavors change often but might include favorites like stracciatella (with chocolate shavings) and hazelnut as well as more unusual flavors like matcha or carrot cake. **Known for:** all natural ingredients; unusual flavors; gluten-free with many vegan options. ⓢ *Average main: €3* ✉ *Piazza degli Zingari, 5, Monti* ☎ *06/48906955* ⊕ *www.gelateriafatamorgana.com* Ⓜ *Cavour.*

★ Zia Rosetta

$ | **SANDWICHES** | Translating to "Aunt Rosetta," the name of this tiny sandwich shop is a play on words, since rosetta is not just a female name but also a type of roll commonly found in Rome. Here the rolls are used to make gourmet sandwiches with delicious combinations of meat, cheeses, veggies, or fish, such as the "Peggy Rockefeller" with prosciutto, crunchy parmigiano reggiano, and eggplant or the "Sora Lella" with anchovies, stracciatella, and puntarelle. **Known for:** gourmet sandwiches; vegan and gluten-free options; seasonal specials. ⓢ *Average main: €7* ✉ *Via Urbana, 54, Monti* ☎ *06/31052516* ⊕ *www.ziarosetta.com* Ⓜ *Cavour.*

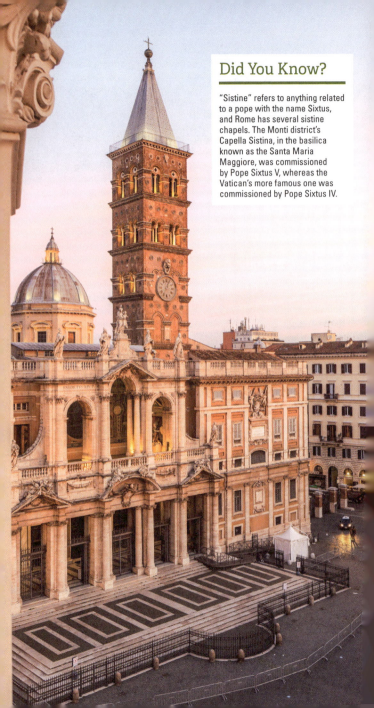

Did You Know?

"Sistine" refers to anything related to a pope with the name Sixtus, and Rome has several sistine chapels. The Monti district's Capella Sistina, in the basilica known as the Santa Maria Maggiore, was commissioned by Pope Sixtus V, whereas the Vatican's more famous one was commissioned by Pope Sixtus IV.

Hotels

Capo d'Africa
$$$ | HOTEL | A great location and amenities, plus outstanding customer service make a stay at this hotel worth every euro. **Pros:** quiet, comfortable rooms; fitness center and rooftop terrace; friendly, welcoming staff. **Cons:** hotel lacks a great view of Colosseum despite proximity; not a lot of restaurants in the immediate neighborhood; Wi-Fi can be spotty. ⑤ *Rooms from: €289* ✉ *Via Capo d'Africa, 54, Celio* ☎ *06/772801* ⊕ *www.hotelcapodafrica.com* ⇌ *65 rooms* ⏺ *No Meals* Ⓜ *Colosseo, Manzoni.*

Hotel Lancelot
$$$ | HOTEL | FAMILY | This friendly home-away-from-home in a quiet residential area close to the Colosseum has been run by the Khan family since 1971. **Pros:** hospitable staff; secluded and quiet; very family-friendly. **Cons:** some bathrooms are on the small side; no in-room refrigerators; some rooms are in need of redecorating. ⑤ *Rooms from: €210* ✉ *Via Capo d'Africa, 47, Celio* ☎ *06/70450615* ⊕ *www.lancelothotel.com* ⇌ *61 rooms* ⏺ *Free Breakfast* Ⓜ *Colosseo.*

Nerva Boutique Hotel
$$$ | HOTEL | Step out of this charming, clean, well-run hotel, and you'll feel like you've landed in the middle of an ancient imperial stomping ground; a stone's throw from the Forum, it's surrounded by the breathtaking splendor of ancient ruins. **Pros:** close to the Forum; friendly staff; modern design. **Cons:** some showers are tiny; single rooms are only slightly bigger than a closet; breakfast not included. ⑤ *Rooms from: €300* ✉ *Via Tor de' Conti, 3/4, Monti* ☎ *06/6781835* ⊕ *www.hotelnerva.com* ⇌ *18 rooms* ⏺ *No Meals* Ⓜ *Cavour, Colosseo.*

NH Collection Roma Fori Imperiali
$$$$ | HOTEL | It would be hard to find a modern hotel closer to the Roman Forum—the ancient ruins are practically right outside the door. **Pros:** incredible views of ancient Rome; rooftop serves a great aperitivo and refined dinners; restaurant Oro Bistrot by renowned chef Natale Giunta. **Cons:** breakfast foods are pre-packaged; not much public space; no spa or gym. ⑤ *Rooms from: €400* ✉ *Via di Santa Eufemia, 19, Monti* ☎ *06/697689911* ⊕ *www.nh-collection.com/en/hotel/nh-collection-roma-fori-imperiali* ⇌ *42 rooms* ⏺ *No Meals* Ⓜ *Colosseo.*

Palazzo Manfredi
$$$$ | **HOTEL** | If you dream of waking up to head-on views of the Colosseum, book into this boutique hotel, which is set in a 17th-century palazzo built over the ruins of the Ludus Magnus, the gymnasium used by Roman gladiators, and offers refined luxury. **Pros:** incredible views; unparalleled location; excellent restaurant and cocktail bar. **Cons:** not all rooms have Colosseum views; some guests complain about noise; no spa. ⑤ *Rooms from: €600* ✉ *Via Labicana, 125, Colosseo* ☎ *06/77591380* ⊕ *www.palazzomanfredi.com* ⇌ *23 rooms* ⓘ◎┃ *No Meals* Ⓜ *Colosseo.*

Palazzo Velabro
$$$$ | **HOTEL** | A member of Design Hotels, this 32-room boutique bolt-hole has spacious rooms and suites, the majority of which come equipped with a kitchenette and sofa bed—some have balconies with views of the Palatine Hill. **Pros:** screening room; spacious rooms and suites; nice restaurant and outdoor bar. **Cons:** rates increase based on occupancy; not many restaurants in the immediate vicinity; no spa. ⑤ *Rooms from: €500* ✉ *Via del Velabro, 16, Aventino* ☎ *06/97619197* ⊕ *www.palazzovelabro.it* ⇌ *32 rooms* ⓘ◎┃ *No Meals* Ⓜ *Circo Massimo.*

Chapter 4

THE VATICAN

4

Updated by
Laura Itzkowitz

◉ Sights	🍴 Restaurants	🛏 Hotels	🛍 Shopping	🍸 Nightlife
★★★★★	★★★☆☆	★★★☆☆	★★☆☆☆	★★☆☆☆

The Vatican Museums Tour

One of the world's largest museum complexes, the Vatican Museums comprise 26 museums, plus various chapels, and receive up to 30,000 visitors per day. Within you'll find Michelangelo's Sistine Chapel and masterpieces of art spanning more than 2,000 years.

1 **After coming through the main entrance, you'll be funneled up an escalator—the only one in the museum. At the top, turn right and head straight out to the Pine Cone Courtyard.** In the center of the courtyard, you can admire Arnaldo Pomodoro's *Sphere within a Sphere*. Abutting the lawn, there are a few panels showing the frescoes in the Sistine Chapel and explaining what they depict and who painted them (Michelangelo only painted the ceiling, not the frescoes on the walls).

2 **Use the doorway on the northwestern side of the courtyard, turn left, and climb a staircase to enter the Pio Clementino Museum,** which houses the most important works of classical sculpture in the pontifical collections. Walk outside into the Octagonal Courtyard and stop to admire the sculpture of Laocöon, which was found on the Esquiline Hill in 1506. It depicts the myth of Laocöon, a Trojan priest who tried to warn his fellow citizens not to accept the wooden horse left by the Greeks, but was attacked by serpents sent by Athena and Poseidon.

Walking Tour 101

HIGHLIGHTS
Laocoön and His Sons, the Belvedere Torso, Gallery of Maps, Raphael Rooms, the Sistine Chapel

WHERE TO START
The Pinecone Courtyard

LENGTH
2 to 3 hours, depending on whether you choose to see the Raphael Rooms

WHERE TO END
The Sistine Chapel

INSIDER TIPS
Be sure to book tickets online in advance or risk wasting half your day waiting in line to get in. To avoid the crowds, go early in the morning or check for evenings when the museum is open late.

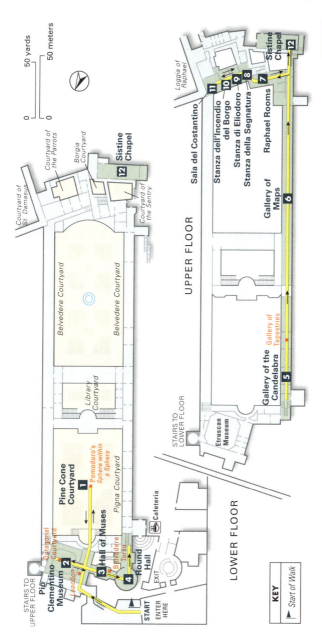

The elaborately decorated ceiling of the Gallery of Maps is a showstopper.

3 Go back inside and enter the Hall of Muses, where you'll see the Belvedere Torso roped off in the center of the room. This fragment of a Greek sculpture was found in Rome at the end of the 15th century and has been admired by artists including Michelangelo as an outstanding example of ancient sculpture. Some scholars have drawn parallels between this sculpture and Michelangelo's depiction of Adam in the Sistine Chapel. The frescoes on the vaulted ceiling represent Apollo and the Muses.

4 Continue on and enter the Round Hall, which has a coffered dome resembling the one at the Pantheon. In the center of the room is an enormous porphyry basin from Nero's Domus Aurea. Note the colossal gilded bronze statue of Heracles, which was discovered in 1864 near Campo de' Fiori, in the area of the ancient Pompey's Theater. It had been struck by lightning and given a ritual burial in the ancient Roman custom.

5 Climb the stairs to the upper floor and you'll come to the Gallery of the Candelabra, named for the massive marble candelabra that, together with the columns, divides the hall into sections. At the end of the gallery, you'll pass through a door and enter the Gallery of Tapestries, whose walls are covered in a series of 16th-century Flemish tapestries depicting the life of Christ.

6 You'll then enter the Gallery of Maps. It displays a series of 40 frescoes depicting maps of the various regions of Italy as they existed during the 16th century, when they were commissioned by Pope Gregory XIII.

On the left side of the room, you can admire the regions on the Tyrrhenian coast, while the maps on the right side depict the Adriatic coast. When you come to the map of Lazio, look at the bottom-left corner, where you can see a blown-up map of Rome.

7 At the end of the Gallery of Maps you have a choice: turn left to see the Raphael Rooms or turn right to skip directly to the Sistine Chapel. The frescoes in the four Raphael rooms were commissioned by Pope Julius II della Rovere to decorate his residence and represent the High Renaissance style.

8 In the first Raphael room, the Stanza della Segnatura, you can admire Raphael's depiction of the School of Athens, which shows ancient Greek philosophers debating the nature of the universe.

9 The second room, the Stanza di Eliodoro, was used as the pope's audience chamber. Here you can see a fresco depicting the expulsion of Heliodorus from the Temple in Jerusalem and the dramatic Liberation of Saint Peter.

10 The third room, the Stanza dell'Incendio del Borgo, was used as the pope's dining room. The frescoes here show a fire raging in the Borgo, the area surrounding the Vatican, in AD 847, with people fleeing the flames as Pope Leo IV appears on the loggia of the old Saint Peter's Basilica to save the day.

11 The last room, the Sala del Costantino, was largely painted by Raphel's students after the master's untimely death in 1520. This room is dedicated to Constantine, the first Christian emperor of Rome.

12 Now it's time to visit the Sistine Chapel, which contains some of the most breathtaking paintings ever created by human hands. The lateral walls were decorated in the 15th century by a team of painters, including Pietro Perugino and Sandro Botticelli, and depict the stories of Moses and of Christ, as well as portraits of the popes. The chapel is named for Pope Sixtus IV della Rovere, but it was Pope Julius II della Rovere who commissioned Michelangelo to paint the ceiling and the Last Judgment on the altar wall. The nine central panels on the ceiling show the story of Genesis, including the famous creation of man.

The Sistine Chapel

NEIGHBORHOOD SNAPSHOT

TOP EXPERIENCES

■ **Michelangelo's Sistine Ceiling:** The most sublime example of artistry in the world, this 10,000-square-foot fresco took the artist four long, neck-craning years to finish.

■ **St. Peter's Dome:** Climb the twisting Renaissance stairs to the top for a well-earned view (the elevator to the right of the main church portico goes up to the base of the dome, but there are still a lot of stairs afterwards).

■ **Papal Blessing:** Join the singing, flag-waving throngs from around the world at the Wednesday general audience on St. Peter's Square (usually only in spring, summer, and early fall).

■ **Musei Vaticani:** Savor one of the Western world's best art collections—from the Apollo Belvedere to Raphael's Transfiguration.

■ **St. Peter's Basilica:** Stand in awe of the largest church in the world.

MAKE THE MOST OF YOUR TIME

The Musei Vaticani are among the most congested of all Rome's attractions. The best way to avoid long lines is to make reservations online for an extra €5 (⊕ *tickets.museivaticani.va/home*). Although reservations do minimize your wait time, it can still be extremely busy once you're inside. The free Sunday is best avoided altogether. Another good idea is to schedule your visit during the Wednesday General Audience, held in the piazza of St. Peter's or at Aula Paolo VI, usually at 9:15 am when the pope is in town. To see the pope's calendar, visit ⊕ *www.papalaudience.org*.

GETTING HERE

■ Metro stops Cipro or Ottaviano will get you within about a 10-minute walk of the entrance to the Musei Vaticani. Or, from Termini station, Bus No. 40 Express or the famously crowded No. 64 will take you to Piazza San Pietro. Both routes swing past Largo Argentina, where you can also get Bus No. 492 or 46.

■ A leisurely meander from the *centro storico* (historic center), across the exquisite Ponte Sant'Angelo, will take about a half hour.

For many, a visit to the Vatican is one of the top reasons to visit Rome, and it is a vast and majestic place, jam-packed with things to see. The Borgo and Prati are the neighborhoods immediately surrounding the Vatican, and it's worth noting that, while the Vatican may well be a priority, these neighborhoods are not the best places to choose a hotel, as they're quite far from other top sights in the city.

The Vatican is an exercise in spirituality, requiring patience but delivering joy. Some come here for a transcendent glimpse of a heavenly Michelangelo fresco; others come in search of a direct connection with the divine. But what all visitors share, for a few hours, is an awe-inspiring landscape that offers a famous sight for every taste: rooms decorated by Raphael, antique sculptures like the *Apollo Belvedere*, famous paintings by Giotto and Bellini, and, perhaps most of all, the Sistine Chapel—for the lover of beauty, few places are as historically important as this epitome of faith and grandeur.

The story of this area's importance dates back to the 1st century, when St. Peter, the first Roman Catholic pope, was buried here. The first basilica in his honor rose on this spot some 250 years later under Emperor Constantine, who legitimized Christianity. It wasn't until the early 15th century, however, that the papacy decided to make this area not only a major spiritual center but the spot from which they would wield temporal power as well.

Today, it's difficult not to be reminded of that worldly power when you take in the massive Renaissance walls surrounding Vatican City—the international boundary of an independent sovereign state, established by the Lateran Treaty of 1929 between the Holy See and Mussolini's government.

Legally recognized as its own city-state, Vatican City covers 110 acres on a hill west of the Tiber and is separated from the city on all sides, except at Piazza di San Pietro, by high walls. Within the walls, about 840 people are permanent residents. The Vatican has its own daily newspaper (*L'Osservatore Romano*), issues its own stamps, mints its own coins, and has its own postal system (run by the Swiss). Within its territory are administrative and foreign offices, a pharmacy, banks, an astronomical observatory, a print shop, a mosaic school and art restoration institute, a tiny train station, a supermarket, a small department store, and several gas stations. The sovereign of the world's smallest state is the pope, Francis, elected in 2013 after his predecessor, Benedict XVI, stepped down (the first time a pope has "resigned" from office since 1415). His main role is as spiritual leader to the world's Catholic community.

Today, there are two principal reasons for sightseeing at the Vatican. One is to visit the Basilica di San Pietro, the most overwhelming architectural achievement of the Renaissance; the other is to visit the Musei Vaticani, which contain collections of staggering richness and diversity, from ancient Etruscan treasures and Egyptian mummies to an actual piece of the Moon.

Inside the basilica—breathtaking both for its sheer size and for its extravagant interior—are artistic masterpieces including Michelangelo's *Pietà* and Bernini's great bronze *baldacchino* (canopy) over the main altar. The Musei Vaticani, a 10-minute walk from the piazza, hold endless collections of many of the greatest works of Western art. The Laocoön, Leonardo's *St. Jerome in the Wilderness*, and Raphael's *Transfiguration* are all here. The Sistine Chapel, accessible only through these museums, is Michelangelo's magnificent artistic legacy, and his ceiling is the High Renaissance in excelsis in more ways than one.

Sights

★ Basilica di San Pietro
CHURCH | The world's largest church, built over the tomb of St. Peter, is the most imposing and breathtaking architectural achievement of the Renaissance (although much of the lavish interior dates to the Baroque period). No fewer than five of Italy's greatest artists—Bramante, Raphael, Peruzzi, Antonio da Sangallo the Younger, and Michelangelo—died while striving to erect this new St. Peter's.

The history of the original St. Peter's goes back to AD 326, when the emperor Constantine completed a basilica over the site of the tomb of St. Peter, the Church's first pope. The original church stood for more than 1,000 years, undergoing a number of restorations and alterations, until, toward the middle of the 15th century, it was on the verge of collapse. In 1452, a reconstruction job began but was abandoned for lack of money.

In 1503, Pope Julius II instructed the architect Bramante to raze all the existing buildings and build a new basilica, one that would surpass even Constantine's for grandeur. It wasn't until 1626 that the new basilica was completed and consecrated.

Highlights include the Loggia delle Benedizioni (Benediction Loggia), the balcony where newly elected popes are proclaimed; Michelangelo's *Pietà*; and Bernini's great bronze baldacchino, a huge, spiral-columned canopy—at 100,000 pounds, perhaps the largest bronze object in the world—as well as many other Bernini masterpieces. There are also collections of Vatican treasures in the Museo Storico-Artistico e Tesoro and the Grotte Vaticane crypt.

For views of both the dome above and the piazza below, take the elevator or stairs to the roof. Those with more stamina (and without claustrophobia) can then head up more stairs to the apex of the dome. ■**TIP→ The basilica is free to visit, but a security check at the entrance can create very long lines. Arrive before 8:30 or after 5:30 to minimize the wait and avoid the crowds.** ✉ *Piazza San Pietro, Vatican* ⊕ *www.vatican.va* 🎫 *Free* ⊗ *Closed during Papal General Audience (Wed. until 1 pm) and during other ceremonies in piazza* Ⓜ *Ottaviano*.

★ Cappella Sistina (*Sistine Chapel*)
ART MUSEUM | In 1508, the redoubtable Pope Julius II commissioned Michelangelo to fresco the more than 10,000 square feet of the Sistine Chapel's ceiling. (*Sistine,* by the way, is simply the adjective form of *Sixtus,* in reference to Pope Sixtus IV, who commissioned the chapel itself.) The task took four years, and it's said that, for many years afterward, Michelangelo couldn't read anything without holding it over his head. The result, however, was the greatest artwork of the Renaissance. A pair of binoculars helps greatly, as does a small mirror—hold it facing the ceiling and look down to study the reflection.

More than 20 years after his work on the ceiling, Michelangelo was called on again, this time by Pope Paul III, to add to the chapel's decoration by painting the *Last Judgment* on the wall over the altar. By way of signature on this, his last great fresco, Michelangelo painted his own face on the flayed-off human skin in St. Bartholomew's hand. ■**TIP→ The chapel is entered through the Musei Vaticani, and lines are slightly shorter after 2:30 (reservations are always advisable)—except free Sundays, which are extremely busy and when admissions close at 12:30.** ✉ *Musei Vaticani, Vatican* ⊕ *www.museivaticani.va* 🎫 *€20 (part of the Vatican Museums)* ⊗ *Closed Sun.* Ⓜ *Ottaviano*.

Castel Sant'Angelo
CASTLE/PALACE | FAMILY | Standing between the Tiber and the Vatican, this circular castle has long been one of Rome's most distinctive landmarks. Opera lovers know it well as the setting for the final scene of Puccini's *Tosca*. Started in AD 135, the structure began as a mausoleum for the emperor Hadrian and was completed by his successor, Antoninus Pius. From the mid-6th century the building became a fortress, a place of refuge for popes during wars and sieges.

Its name dates to AD 590, when Pope Gregory the Great, during a procession to plead for the end of a plague, saw an angel standing on the summit of the castle, sheathing his sword. Taking this as a sign that the plague was at an end, the pope built a small chapel at the top, placing a statue next to it to celebrate his vision—thus the name, Castel Sant'Angelo.

In the rooms off the Cortile dell'Angelo, look for the Cappella di Papa Leone X (Chapel of Pope Leo X), with a facade by Michelangelo. In the Pope Alexander VI courtyard, a wellhead bears the Borgia coat of arms. The stairs at the far end of the courtyard lead to the open terrace for a view of the Passetto, the fortified corridor connecting Castel Sant'Angelo with the Vatican. In the *appartamento papale* (papal apartment), the Sala Paolina (Pauline Room) was decorated in the 16th century by Perino del Vaga and assistants with lavish frescoes of scenes from the Old Testament and the lives of St. Paul and Alexander the Great. ✉ *Lungotevere Castello, 50, Prati* ☎ *06/6819111 central line, 06/6896003 tickets* ⊕ *www.castelsantangelo.beniculturali.it* 🎫 *€13* ⊗ *Closed Mon.* Ⓜ *Lepanto.*

★ **Musei Vaticani** (*Vatican Museums*)
ART MUSEUM | Other than the pope and his papal court, the occupants of the Vatican are some of the most famous artworks in the world. The Vatican Palace, residence of the popes since 1377, consists of an estimated 1,400 rooms, chapels, and galleries. The pope and his household occupy only a small part; most of the rest is given over to the Vatican Library and Museums.

Beyond the glories of the Sistine Chapel, the collection is extraordinarily rich: highlights include the great antique sculptures (including the celebrated *Apollo Belvedere* in the Octagonal Courtyard and the *Belvedere Torso* in the Hall of the Muses); the Stanze di Raffaello (Raphael Rooms), with their famous gorgeous frescoes; and the Old Master paintings, such as Leonardo da Vinci's beautiful (though unfinished) *St. Jerome in the Wilderness*, some of Raphael's greatest creations, and Caravaggio's gigantic *Deposition in the Pinacoteca* ("Picture Gallery").

For those interested in guided visits to the Vatican Museums, tours start at €40, including entrance tickets, and can also be booked online. Other offerings include a regular two-hour guided tour of the Vatican gardens; call or check online to confirm. For more information, call ☎ *06/69884676* or go to ⊕ *www.museivaticani.va*. For information on tours, call ☎ *06/69883145* or ☎ *06/69884676;* visually impaired visitors can arrange tactile tours by calling ☎ *06/69884947.* ✉ *Viale Vaticano, near intersection with Via Leone IV, Vatican* ☎ *06/69883145* ⊕ *www.museivaticani.va* 💶 *€20* ⊘ *Closed Sun. and church holidays* Ⓜ *Cipro–Musei Vaticani or Ottaviano–San Pietro.*

★ Piazza San Pietro

PLAZA/SQUARE | Mostly enclosed within high walls that recall the papacy's stormy history, the Vatican opens the spectacular arms of Bernini's colonnade to embrace the world only at St. Peter's Square, scene of the pope's public appearances and another of Bernini's masterpieces. The elliptical Piazza di San Pietro was completed in 1667—after only 11 years' work—and holds about 100,000 people.

Surrounded by a pair of quadruple colonnades, the piazza is gloriously studded with 140 statues of saints and martyrs. At its center is the 85-foot-high Egyptian obelisk, which was brought to Rome by Caligula in AD 37 and moved here in 1586 by Pope Sixtus V. The famous Vatican post offices can be found on both sides of St. Peter's Square and inside the Vatican Museums complex. ■**TIP**➜ **The main information office is just left of the basilica as you face it.** ✉ *Piazza di San Pietro, Vatican* ⊕ *www.vaticanstate.va* Ⓜ *Ottaviano.*

Ponte Sant'Angelo

BRIDGE | Angels designed by Baroque master Bernini line the most beautiful of central Rome's 20-odd bridges. Bernini himself carved only two of the angels (those with the scroll and the crown of thorns), both of which were moved to the church of Sant'Andrea delle Fratte shortly afterward at the behest of the Bernini family. Though copies, the angels on the bridge today convey forcefully the grace and characteristic sense of movement—a key element of Baroque sculpture—of Bernini's best work.

Originally built in AD 133–134, the Ponte Elio, as it was originally called, was a bridge over the Tiber to Hadrian's Mausoleum. Pope Gregory changed the bridge's name after he had a vision of an angel sheathing its sword to signal the ending of the plague of 590. In medieval times, continuing its sacral function, the bridge became an important element in funneling pilgrims toward St. Peter's. As such, in 1667 Pope Clement IX commissioned Bernini

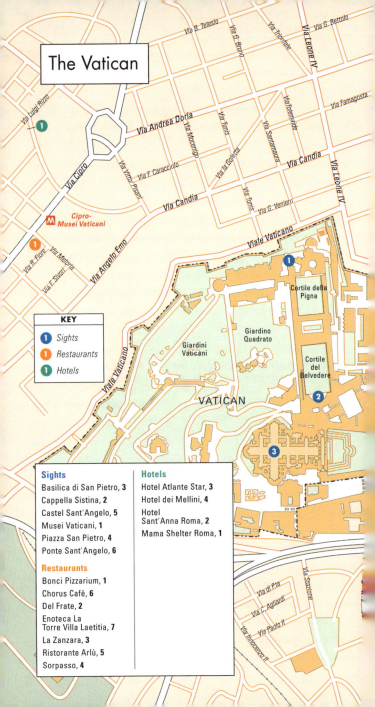

to design 10 angels bearing the symbols of the Passion, turning the bridge into a sort of Via Crucis. ✉ *Between Lungotevere Castello and Lungotevere Altoviti, Borgo* Ⓜ *Ottaviano.*

🍴 Restaurants

★ Bonci Pizzarium
$ | PIZZA | FAMILY | This tiny storefront by famed pizzaiolo Gabriele Bonci is the city's most famous place for pizza *al taglio* (by the slice). It serves more than a dozen versions, from the standard margherita to slices piled high with prosciutto and other tasty ingredients. **Known for:** Rome's best pizza al taglio; over a dozen flavors; long lines. 💲 *Average main: €5* ✉ *Via della Meloria, 43, Prati* ☎ *06/39745416* ⊕ *www.bonci.it* ⊗ *Closed Mon.* Ⓜ *Cipro.*

★ Chorus Café
$$ | MODERN ITALIAN | Tucked away above the Auditorium della Conciliazione, this glamorous restaurant/lounge with sky-high ceilings, marble walls, and plush seating feels like something out of Paolo Sorrentino's award-winning film *La Grande Bellezza*. Renowned bartender Massimo d'Addezio shakes up creative cocktails, like a twist on a French 75 made with yuzu, while the kitchen whips up delicious modern Italian cuisine. **Known for:** top-notch cocktails; sumptuous surroundings; DJ sets on the weekends. 💲 *Average main: €23* ✉ *Auditorium della Conciliazione, Via della Conciliazione, 4, Borgo* ☎ *335/1449655* ⊕ *www.choruscafe.it* ⊗ *Closed Sun. and Mon.* Ⓜ *Ottaviano.*

Del Frate
$$ | MODERN ITALIAN | This impressive wine bar pairs modern decor with creative cuisine and three dozen wines available by the glass. There are some fantastic seasonal specialties, but you can also get cheeses, smoked meats, and composed salads. **Known for:** shares space with one of Rome's noted wine shops; daily aperitivo with a nice selection of wines by the glass; wide selection of after-dinner drinks, including mezcal and amari (bitter cordial). 💲 *Average main: €24* ✉ *Via degli Scipioni, 118, Prati* ☎ *06/3236437* ⊕ *www.enotecadelfrate.it* ⊗ *Closed 2 wks in Aug.* Ⓜ *Ottaviano.*

★ Enoteca La Torre Villa Laetitia
$$$$ | MODERN ITALIAN | In the Villa Laetitia, a boutique hotel owned by the Fendi family, this gorgeous restaurant has soaring ceilings, a crystal chandelier, and Art Nouveau motifs. The elegant setting provides the perfect backdrop for creative, flavorful dishes by Domenico Stile, one of Rome's youngest two-Michelin-starred chefs. **Known for:** one of the most beautiful restaurants in Rome; flavorful, creative cuisine; creative wine pairings. 💲 *Average*

For St. Peter's, Michelangelo originally designed a dome much higher than the one ultimately completed by his follower, Giacomo della Porta.

main: €40 ✉ *Villa Laetitia, Lungotevere delle Armi, 23, Prati* ☎ *06/45668304* ⊕ *www.enotecalatorreroma.com* ⊙ *Closed Mon. and Tues.* Ⓜ *Lepanto.*

La Zanzara

$$$ | **INTERNATIONAL** | This bright, modern establishment functions as a bar, café, and restaurant all in one, with plenty of indoor and outdoor seating. Salads, pastas, steaks, and seafood run the international gamut, but the beef burger is a standout. **Known for:** bacon cheeseburger; artisanal Italian beers; large grill for freshly cooked meats. ⓢ *Average main: €26* ✉ *Via Crescenzio, 84, Prati* ☎ *06/68392227* ⊕ *www.lazanzararoma.com* Ⓜ *Ottaviano.*

Ristorante Arlù

$$$ | **MODERN ITALIAN** | This tiny family-run restaurant has changed a lot since it first opened in 1959 as a simple trattoria. Today you'll still find classic Roman dishes on the menu, but it's worth trying original creations like salmon marinated in Aperol with avocado and savory panna cotta or the homemade ravioli stuffed with ricotta and topped with octopus confit. **Known for:** historic family-run restaurant; elegant decor; creative and classic dishes. ⓢ *Average main: €28* ✉ *Borgo Pio, 135, Borgo* ☎ *06/68689936* ⊕ *www.ristorantearlu.it* Ⓜ *Ottaviano.*

Sorpasso

$$ | **MODERN ITALIAN** | **FAMILY** | The focus at this happening spot is on using excellently sourced products to make simple but wonderful food. In the morning and afternoon, stop in for freshly

baked sweet treats; in the evening, when people spill out into the street with cocktails in hand, come for an aperitivo or a hearty meal. **Known for:** meat and cheese board; strozzapretti (a short pasta) served with eggplant, pistachio, and chili bread crumbs; juicy steaks. ⑤ *Average main: €15* ✉ *Via Properzio, 31–33, Prati* ☎ *06/89024554* ⊕ *sorpasso.info/home-page* ☾ *Closed Sun. and Aug.* Ⓜ *Ottaviano.*

Hotels

Hotel Atlante Star

$$$ | HOTEL | The rooftop garden terrace with a center-stage view of St. Peter's Basilica is just one reason to stay here; proximity to the Vatican and superb shopping is another. **Pros:** all rooms have robes and amenity kits; panoramic roof garden and terrace is open from morning to night; restaurant serves sophisticated cuisine with beautiful views. **Cons:** some rooms are nicer than others; one of the elevators is on the small side and a bit slow; some furniture and fixtures are in need of upgrading. ⑤ *Rooms from: €230* ✉ *Via Vitelleschi, 34, Borgo* ☎ *06/686386* ⊕ *www.atlantehotels.com* ⇨ *65 rooms* ⑩ *Free Breakfast* Ⓜ *Ottaviano.*

Hotel dei Mellini

$$ | HOTEL | On the west bank of the Tiber between the Spanish Steps and St. Peter's Basilica (a 10-minute stroll from Piazza del Popolo and the nearest Metro station), this modern luxury hotel is removed from the chaos of the centro storico. **Pros:** spacious and spotless rooms; breakfast served until 11 am; free bicycles to use based on availability. **Cons:** not for those who want to be in the center of the action; few dining options right nearby; spotty cell service. ⑤ *Rooms from: €149* ✉ *Via Muzio Clementi, 81, Prati* ☎ *06/324771* ⊕ *www.hotelmellini.com* ⇨ *81 rooms* ⑩ *Free Breakfast* Ⓜ *Lepanto, Flaminio.*

Hotel Sant'Anna Roma

$ | HOTEL | Set in the shadow of St. Peter's, this small hotel is a good value, with simply decorated, ample guest rooms that feature wood-beam ceilings, parquet floors, and comfy beds. **Pros:** street is a pedestrian-only zone; beds are comfy; staff are friendly. **Cons:** no on-site bar or restaurant, and many nearby restaurants are tourist traps; the neighborhood is dead at night; they can charge extra for a late checkout. ⑤ *Rooms from: €120* ✉ *Borgo Pio, 133, Borgo* ☎ *06/68801602* ⊕ *www.santannahotel.net* ⇨ *20 rooms* ⑩ *Free Breakfast* Ⓜ *Ottaviano.*

Did You Know?

Designed to be Hadrian's tomb, the Castel Sant'Angelo was originally topped by a marble-sheathed tumulus and crowned by a gigantic bronze of the emperor in his chariot.

★ Mama Shelter Roma

$$ | **HOTEL** | **FAMILY** | The first Italian outpost of the French brand, Mama Shelter, this hip hotel features a funky design with lots colors and patterns and playful touches like graphic ceilings painted by French street artist Beniloys and vintage pinball machines you can play. **Pros:** sex-positive and LGBTQ+ friendly; programming like beer tastings and weekend brunch; relaxing area with a pool, sauna, and gym. **Cons:** breakfast buffet costs €22; a bit far from most of the major sights; €25 cleaning fee for pets.
⑤ *Rooms from: €149* ✉ *Via Luigi Rizzo, 20, Prati* ☎ *06/94538900* ⊕ *www.mamashelter.com/roma* ⇨ *217 rooms* ⊚ *No Meals* Ⓜ *Cipro.*

Chapter 5

PIAZZA NAVONA, CAMPO DE' FIORI, AND THE JEWISH GHETTO

Updated by
Laura Itzkowitz

 Sights   Restaurants   Hotels   Shopping   Nightlife

★★★★★   ★★★☆☆   ★★★★★   ★★★★☆   ★★★★☆

Piazza Navona, Campo de' Fiori, and the Jewish Ghetto Walking Tour

The heart of Rome's historic center is concentrated in this area, which extends from the Pantheon to the Tiber River. Here you'll find some of the city's most scenic piazzas, palaces, churches, and cobblestone streets that invite you to wander.

1 **If you want to start the tour with a pick-me-up, pop into the historic Tazza d'Oro** for an espresso, cappuccino, or their signature *granita di caffè con panna* (a sort of coffee slushie with whipped cream).

2 **Walk over to one of the city's most famous sights: the Pantheon.** Rome's best preserved ancient temple, the Pantheon was first constructed in 27 BC by Augustus Caesar's son-in-law Agrippa, then rebuilt in AD 120 by Hadrian before being converted into a church in AD 608 (hence why it was preserved). The awe-inspiring building has a height that's perfectly equal to the diameter of its dome and houses the tombs of Raphael and Victor Emanuel II, the first king of Italy. As of 2024, you must buy a €5 ticket to enter, which you can book online in advance if you want to avoid the line. Spend some time lingering on the beautiful Piazza del Pantheon and admiring the fountain topped with an obelisk in the middle.

Walking Tour 101

HIGHLIGHTS
The Pantheon, San Luigi dei Francesi, Piazza Navona, Santa Maria della Pace, Via Giulia, Palazzo Farnese, Piazza Campo de' Fiori, Portico d'Ottavia, Sinagoga

WHERE TO START
Tazza d'Oro

LENGTH
1-2 hours, depending on your pace and how often you stop

WHERE TO END
Sinagoga

BEST TIME TO GO
Weekday mornings, when the market in Campo de' Fiori and Pasticceria Boccione are open

WORST TIME TO GO
On a rainy day

The market on Campo de' Fiori is a popular morning stop to pick up fresh produce.

3 **Walk west and you'll encounter San Luigi dei Francesi.** This magnificent church is worth a stop to peek at the three incredible paintings by Caravaggio, the master of *chiaroscuro*, in the Contarelli Chapel.

4 **Continue west and within a couple of minutes you'll arrive at Piazza Navona,** which unfolds like a Baroque fever dream before your eyes. Built over the ruins of an ancient racetrack, the long, oval piazza is widely considered Rome's most spectacular Baroque square. Stop to admire Bernini's Fountain of the Four Rivers in the middle of the piazza. The four figures represent the longest rivers of the known continents in 1651, when Bernini designed the fountain: the Nile, the Ganges, the Danube, and the Plata.

5 **Continue walking west on Via di Sant'Agnese in Agone, then turn right on Via della Pace.** At the end of the street is the tiny Church of Santa Maria della Pace. Peek inside to see Raphael's Sibyls above the first altar on the right.

6 **Exit the church, turn right, walk past the Chiostro del Bramante, then make a left on Via dei Coronari.** Here you'll find the enticing Gelateria del Teatro, where you can stop for a gelato.

7 **Stroll west on Via dei Coronari, turn left on Via del Panico, then right on Vicolo della Campanella.** Cross the busy Corso Vittorio Emanuele II, then follow Vicolo delle Palle until you reach Via Giulia. One of Rome's most elegant thoroughfares, Via Giulia was named for Pope Julius II, who commissioned it during the Renaissance. It's a pleasure to stroll along this cobblestone street lined with palaces, churches, and restaurants. You will pass under the arch designed by Michelangelo, which was meant to link Palazzo Farnese to the Villa Farnesina across the river in Trastevere. Just past the arch, note the Fontana del Mascherone on the right.

8 Turn left on Via del Mascherone and you'll arrive at Piazza Farnese. This elegant square is home to Palazzo Farnese (now the French Embassy).

9 The next piazza over is Piazza Campo de' Fiori. If you happen to be here in the morning, you'll want to explore the market on Piazza Campo de' Fiori, believed to be the oldest market in Rome. Some of the stalls have been taken over by vendors hawking limoncello and spice mixes to tourists, but there are still vendors selling fresh local fruit and vegetables to the city's chefs and home cooks. In the evening, after the vendors leave, the area becomes a magnet for exchange students and expats who hang out at the bars on the square. The surrounding streets are lined with shops.

10 Walk east along Via dei Giubbonari, past the little park on Largo Arenula, and cross Via Arenula to get to the Jewish Ghetto. For around 300 years, Rome's Jews lived in this small area under lock and key, leaving in the morning to go to work and returning before the nightly curfew. That ended in 1870 under Italian unification, but today the area is still the spiritual home of Rome's Jewish community. Walk along the main drag, Via del Portico d'Ottavia, and you'll see restaurants (some kosher) serving specialties like *carciofi alla giudea* (fried artichokes), Judaica shops, and bakeries.

11 Though unmarked, you'll recognize Pasticceria Boccione by the line going out the door. Stop here for its *crostata ricotta e visciole* (ricotta and cherry pie), if they still have any available. The popular sweet tends to sell out in the morning.

12 Toward the end of the street you'll see the Portico d'Ottavia, an entrance to a colonnaded walkway that once enclosed two temples, a meeting hall, and a library. Just past the site is the Sinagoga, which houses the Jewish Museum that chronicles the heritage of Rome's Jewish community.

The Pantheon

NEIGHBORHOOD SNAPSHOT

TOP EXPERIENCES

■ **Piazza Navona:** Rome's exuberant Baroque era is on display in this glorious piazza. Admire both Bernini's fountain and Borromini's church of Sant'Agnese.

■ **Caravaggio:** Marvel at the play of light and dark in three of the finest paintings by 17th-century Rome's rebel artist at the church of San Luigi dei Francesi.

■ **The Pantheon:** Gaze up to the heavens through the dome of this ancient temple—is this the world's only architecturally perfect building?

■ **Piazza Campo de' Fiori:** Stroll through the morning market for a taste of la dolce vita. After the sun sets, the area becomes a buzzing meeting place.

■ **Portico d'Ottavia:** Named by Emperor Augustus in honor of his sister Octavia, this famed ancient landmark casts a spell over Rome's Jewish Ghetto.

GETTING HERE

■ Piazza Navona and Campo de' Fiori are an easy walk from the Vatican or Trastevere and a half-hour stroll from the Spanish Steps. From Termini or the Vatican, take Bus No. 40 Express or the No. 64 to Largo Torre Argentina; then walk 10 minutes to either piazza. Bus No. 116 winds from Via Veneto past the Spanish Steps to Campo de' Fiori.

■ From the Vatican or the Spanish Steps, it's a 30-minute walk to the Jewish Ghetto, or take the No. 40 Express or the No. 64 bus from Termini station to Largo Torre Argentina.

The area around Piazza Navona, Campo de' Fiori, and the Jewish Ghetto, also known as the Campo Marzio (Field of Mars) for its military past, is beautiful, atmospheric, and lively. It's a neighborhood that's worth getting lost in, featuring cobblestone side streets and artisans' shops just around the corner from the piazzas, as well as tourist-packed sights and the establishments that cater to them.

In terms of sheer sensual enjoyment—from ornate palaces to mouthwatering restaurants and cozy bars to charming stores—it's tough to top the area north of Corso Vittorio Emanuele II. Just a few blocks (and some 1,200 years) separate the two showstoppers: Piazza Navona and the Pantheon. The first is an extraordinarily beautiful Baroque piazza that serves as the open-air salon for this quarter of Rome. Across Corso di Rinascimento is the Pantheon, the grandest extant building from ancient Rome, topped by the world's largest unreinforced concrete dome. Near the same massive hub, Bernini's delightful elephant obelisk proves that small can also be beautiful.

South of Corso Vittorio Emanuele II, Campo de' Fiori, an evocative piazza ringed by medieval palazzi, is the site of a popular market in the morning—a bustling and beloved *centro storico* institution, where bag-toting *nonnas* shop for daily provisions side by side with people from tour groups browsing for souvenirs. In the evening and until well past midnight, the square is a hot spot, where young Romans and visitors alike patronize outdoor bars and restaurants.

Farther east lies the Jewish Ghetto, established by papal decree in the 16th century. This neighborhood was, by definition, a closed community whose inhabitants lived under lock and key until Italian unification in 1870. In 1943–44, the already small Jewish population was decimated by deportations. Today, most of Rome's Jews live outside the Ghetto, but the area around the city's Great Synagogue is still the community's spiritual and cultural home. That heritage permeates its small commercial district of Judaica shops, kosher bakeries, and restaurants. Note, however, that most businesses here observe the Jewish Sabbath, so it's a relative ghost town on Saturday.

Tight, teeming alleys run down into the Ghetto from Giacomo della Porta's unmistakable Fontana delle Tartarughe (Turtle Fountain). A visit to the turn-of-the-20th-century synagogue, with its museum dedicated to the history of Jewish Rome, is a must for understanding the Ghetto. Afterward, stroll Via Portico d'Ottavia and see its namesake structure in the center of the district. The east end of the street leads down to a path past the 1st-century Teatro di Marcello.

Sights

★ Mercato Campagna Amica
MARKET | FAMILY | On the weekends, Romans and expats alike head to the Mercato Campagna Amica, the city's largest farmers' market. The operation attracts producers from around the Lazio region to sell local cheeses like the hard-to-find *marzolino* cheese, a vast variety of fresh produce, bread made from stone-ground wheat, and salumi (cured meats) galore. Keep an eye out for local pecorino and extra-virgin olive oil. A small kitchen near the back door whips up lunch with seasonal ingredients for about €8, and there is ample outdoor seating. ✉ *Via di S. Teodoro, 74, Jewish Ghetto* ⊕ *mercatocircomassimo.campagnamica.it* ⊙ *Closed weekdays.*

★ Palazzo Altemps
CASTLE/PALACE | Containing some of the world's finest ancient Roman statues, Palazzo Altemps is part of the Museo Nazionale Romano. The palace's sober exterior belies a magnificence that appears as soon as you walk into the majestic courtyard, studded with statues and covered in part by a retractable awning. The restored interior hints at the Roman lifestyle of the 16th–18th centuries while showcasing the most illustrious pieces from the Museo Nazionale, including the collection of the Ludovisi noble family.

In the frescoed salons you can see the *Galata Suicida,* a poignant sculptural work portraying a barbarian warrior who chooses death for himself and his wife rather than humiliation by the enemy. Another highlight is the large Ludovisi sarcophagus, magnificently carved from marble. In a place of honor is the *Ludovisi Throne*, which shows a goddess emerging from the sea and being helped by her acolytes. For centuries this was heralded as one of the most sublime Greek sculptures, but, today, at least one

Every year on the feast of Pentecost, rose petals flutter down the oculus of the Pantheon.

authoritative art historian considers it a colossally overrated fake. Look for the framed explanations of the exhibits that detail (in English) how and exactly where Renaissance sculptors, Bernini among them, added missing pieces to the classical works.

In the lavishly frescoed loggia stand busts of the Caesars. In the wing once occupied by early-20th-century poet Gabriele d'Annunzio (who married into the Altemps family), three rooms host the museum's Egyptian collection. ✉ *Piazza di Sant'Apollinare, 46, Piazza Navona* ☎ *06/684851* ⊕ *museonazionaleromano.beniculturali.it* 🎫 *€8; €12 combined ticket includes three other Museo Nazionale Romano sites over 1 week (Crypta Balbi, Palazzo Massimo alle Terme, and Museo delle Terme di Diocleziano)* ⊗ *Closed Mon.*

★ Pantheon

RELIGIOUS BUILDING | The city's best-preserved ancient building, this former Roman temple is a marvel of architectural harmony and proportion. It was entirely rebuilt by the emperor Hadrian around AD 120 on the site of a Pantheon (from the Greek: *pan,* all, and *theon,* gods) erected in 27 BC by Augustus's right-hand man and son-in-law, Agrippa.

The most striking thing about the Pantheon is not its size, immense though it is, nor even the phenomenal technical difficulties posed by so massive a construction; rather, it's the remarkable unity of the building. The diameter described by the dome is exactly equal to its height. It's the use of such simple mathematical balance that gives classical architecture its characteristic

sense of proportion and its nobility. The opening at the apex of the dome, the *oculus,* is nearly 30 feet in diameter and was intended to symbolize the "all-seeing eye of the heavens." On a practical note, this means when it rains, it rains inside: look out for the drainage holes in the floor.

Although little is known for sure about the Pantheon's origins or purpose, it's worth noting that the five levels of trapezoidal coffers (sunken panels in the ceiling) represent the course of the five then-known planets and their concentric spheres. Ruling over them is the sun, represented symbolically and literally by the 30-foot-wide eye at the top. The heavenly symmetry is further paralleled by the coffers: 28 to each row, the number of lunar cycles. In the center of each would have shone a small bronze star. Down below, the seven large niches were occupied not by saints, but, it's thought, by statues of Mars, Venus, the deified Caesar, and the other "astral deities," including the moon and sun, the "sol invictus." (Academics still argue, however, about which gods were most probably worshipped here.)

One of the reasons the Pantheon is so well preserved is that it was consecrated as a church in AD 608. (It's still a working church today.) No building, church or not, though, escaped some degree of plundering through the turbulent centuries of Rome's history after the fall of the empire. In 655, for example, the gilded bronze covering the dome was stripped. The Pantheon is also one of the city's important burial places. Its most famous tomb is that of Raphael (between the second and third chapels on the left as you enter). Mass takes place on Sunday and on religious holidays at 10:30; it's open to the public, but you are expected to arrive before the beginning and stay until the end. General access usually resumes at about 11:30. You can buy tickets online in advance, which requires registering for an account, but it is better than waiting in the long line at the door. Each reservation can book up to 25 tickets. ■**TIP→ On the first Sunday of every month, visitors can enter for free.** ✉ *Piazza della Rotonda, Piazza Navona* ☎ *06/68300230* ⊕ *www.museiitaliani.it* 🎟 *€5; audio guide €8.50.*

Piazza Campo de' Fiori

MARKET | FAMILY | A bustling marketplace in the morning (Monday through Saturday from 8 to 2) and a trendy meeting place the rest of the day and night, this piazza has plenty of down-to-earth charm. Just after lunchtime, all the fruit and vegetable vendors disappear, and this so-called *piazza trasformista* takes on another identity, becoming a circus of bars particularly favored by study-abroad students, tourists, and young expats. Brooding over the piazza is a hooded statue of the philosopher Giordano Bruno, who was burned at the stake here in 1600 for heresy, one of many victims of the Roman Inquisition. ⊠ *Intersection of Via dei Baullari, Via Giubbonari, Via del Pellegrino, and Piazza della Cancelleria, Campo de' Fiori.*

★ Piazza Navona

PLAZA/SQUARE | Always camera-ready, this beautiful plaza has Bernini sculptures, three gorgeous fountains, and a magnificently Baroque church (Sant'Agnese in Agone), all built atop the remains of a Roman athletics track. Pieces of the arena are still visible near the adjacent Piazza Sant'Apollinare, and the ancient spirit of entertainment lives on in the buskers and artists who populate the piazza today.

The piazza took on its current look during the 17th century, after Pope Innocent X of the Pamphilj family decided to make over his family palace (now the Brazilian embassy and an ultra-luxe hotel) and its surroundings. Center stage is the Fontana dei Quattro Fiumi, created for Innocent by Bernini in 1651. Bernini's powerful figures of the four rivers represent the longest rivers of the known continents at the time: the Nile (his head covered because the source was unknown); the Ganges; the Danube; and the Plata (the length of the Amazon was then unknown). Popular legend has it that the figure of the Plata—the figure closest to Sant'Agnese in Agone—raises his hand before his eyes because he can't bear to look upon the church's "inferior" facade designed by Francesco Borromini, Bernini's rival.

If you want a caffè with one of the most beautiful, if pricey, views in Rome, grab a seat at Piazza Navona. Just be aware that all the restaurants here are heavily geared toward tourists, so while it's a beautiful place for a coffee, you can find cheaper, more authentic, and far better meals elsewhere. ⊠ *Piazza Navona.*

Portico d'Ottavia

RUINS | Looming over the Jewish Ghetto, this huge portico, with a few surviving columns, is one of the area's most picturesque set pieces, with the church of Sant'Angelo in Pescheria built right into its ruins. Named by Augustus in honor of his sister Octavia, it was originally 390 feet wide and 433 feet long; encompassed two temples, a meeting hall, and a library; and served as a kind of grandiose entrance foyer for the adjacent Teatro di Marcello.

In the Middle Ages, the cool marble ruins of the portico became Rome's *pescheria* (fish market). A stone plaque on a pillar (it's a copy as the original is in the Musei Capitolini) states in Latin that the head of any fish surpassing the length of the plaque was to be cut off "up to the first fin" and given to the city fathers or else the vendor was to pay a fine of 10 gold florins. The heads, which were used to make fish soup, were considered a great delicacy. ✉ *Via Portico d'Ottavia, 29, Jewish Ghetto* ☎ *06/0608.*

★ San Luigi dei Francesi

CHURCH | San Luigi's Contarelli Chapel (the fifth and last chapel on the left, toward the main altar) is adorned with three stunningly dramatic works by Caravaggio (1571–1610), the Baroque master of the heightened approach to light and dark. They were commissioned for the tomb of Mattheiu Cointerel in one of Rome's French churches (San Luigi is St. Louis, patron saint of France). The inevitable coin machine will light up his *Calling of Saint Matthew, Saint Matthew and the Angel,* and *Martyrdom of Saint Matthew* (seen from left to right), and Caravaggio's mastery of light takes it from there.

When painted, they caused considerable consternation among the clergy of San Luigi, who thought the artist's dramatically realistic approach was scandalously disrespectful. A first version of the altarpiece was rejected; the priests were not particularly happy with the other two, either. Time has fully vindicated Caravaggio's patron, Cardinal Francesco del Monte, who secured the commission for these works and staunchly defended them. ■**TIP→ This church regularly enforces the rule of covered knees and shoulders, and turns away those who do not abide.** ✉ *Piazza di San Luigi dei Francesi, Piazza Navona* ☎ *06/688271* ⊕ *saintlouis-rome.net.*

Santa Maria della Pace

CHURCH | In 1656, Pietro da Cortona (1596–1669) was commissioned by Pope Alexander VII to enlarge the tiny Piazza della Pace in front of the 15th-century church of Santa Maria so that it could accommodate the carriages of its wealthy parishioners. His architectural solution was to design a new church facade complete with semicircular portico, demolish a few buildings here and there to create a more spacious approach, add arches to give architectural unity to the piazza, and then complete it with a series of bijou-size palaces. The result was one of Rome's most delightful little architectural set pieces.

Within are several great Renaissance treasures. Raphael's fresco above the first altar on your right depicts the *Four Sibyls*—almost exact replicas of Michelangelo's, if more relaxed. The fine decorations of the Cesi Chapel, second on the right, were designed in the mid-16th century by Sangallo. Opposite is Peruzzi's wonderful fresco of the *Madonna and Child.* The octagon below the dome is something of an art gallery in itself, with works by Cavalliere Arpino, Orazio Gentileschi, and others; Cozzo's *Eternity* fills the lantern above.

Behind the church is its cloister, designed by Bramante (architect of St. Peter's) as the very first expression of High Renaissance style in Rome. In addition to an exhibit space for contemporary art, the cloister has a lovely coffee bar. ✉ *Via Arco della Pace, 5, Piazza Navona* ☎ *06/68804038* Ⓜ *Bus Nos. 87, 40, and 64.*

Sinagoga

RELIGIOUS BUILDING | This synagogue has been the city's largest Jewish temple, and a Roman landmark with its distinctive aluminum dome, since its construction in 1904. The building also houses the Jewish Museum, with displays of precious ritual objects and exhibits that document the uninterrupted presence of a Jewish community in the city for nearly 22 centuries. Until the 16th century, Jews were esteemed citizens of Rome. Among them were bankers and physicians to the popes, who had themselves given permission for the construction of synagogues. But, in 1555, during the Counter-Reformation, Pope Paul IV decreed the building of the walls of the Ghetto, confining the Jews to this small flood-prone area and imposing restrictions, some of which continued to be enforced until 1870. For security reasons, entrance is via guided visit only, and tours in English are available twice a day but should be booked online ahead of time. Entrance to the synagogue is through the museum on Via Catalana. ✉ *Lungotevere de' Cenci, 15, Jewish Ghetto* ☎ *06/68400661* ⊕ *www.museoebraico.roma.it* 💶 *€11* ⊘ *Museum closed Sat. and Jewish holidays.*

★ Via Giulia

STREET | Straight as a die and still something of a Renaissance-era diorama, Via Giulia was the first street in Rome since ancient times to be deliberately planned. It was named for Pope Julius II (of Sistine Chapel fame), who commissioned it in the early 1500s as part of a scheme to open up a grandiose approach to St. Peter's Basilica. Although the pope's plans were only partially completed, Via Giulia became an important thoroughfare in Renaissance Rome. It's still, after more than four centuries, the address of choice for Roman aristocrats, despite a recent, controversial addition: a large parking lot along one side of the street (creating it meant steamrolling through ancient and medieval ruins underneath).

A stroll around and along Via Giulia reveals elegant palaces and churches, including one, **San Eligio**, on the little side street Via di Sant'Eligio, that was designed by Raphael himself. Note also the **Palazzo Sacchetti** (✉ *Via Giulia, 66*), with an imposing stone portal and an interior containing some of Rome's grandest staterooms; it remains, after 300 years, the private quarters of the Marchesi

Sacchetti. The forbidding brick building that housed the **Carceri Nuove (New Prison)** (✉ *Via Giulia, 52*), Rome's prison for more than two centuries, now contains the offices of the Direzione Nazionale Antimafia. Near the bridge that arches over Via Giulia's southern end is the church of **Santa Maria dell'Orazione e Morte** (Holy Mary of Prayer and Death), with stone skulls on its door. These are a symbol of a confraternity that was charged with burying the bodies of the unidentified dead found in the city streets.

Designed by Borromini and home, since 1927, to the Hungarian Academy, the **Palazzo Falconieri** (✉ *Via Giulia, 1* ☏ *06/68896700*) has Borromini-designed salons and loggia that are sporadically open as part of guided tours; call for information. The falcon statues atop its belvedere are best viewed from around the block, along the Tiber embankment. Remnant of a master plan by Michelangelo, the arch over the street was meant to link massive **Palazzo Farnese,** on the east side of Via Giulia, with the building across the street and a bridge to the Villa Farnesina, directly across the river. Finally, on the right and rather green with age, dribbles that star of many a postcard, the **Fontana del Mascherone.** ✉ *Via Giulia, between Piazza dell'Oro and Piazza San Vincenzo Palloti, Campo de' Fiori.*

🍴 Restaurants

★ Armando al Pantheon

$$ | **ROMAN** | In the shadow of the Pantheon, this small family-run trattoria, open since 1961, delights tourists and locals alike. There's an air of authenticity to the Roman staples here, and the quality of the ingredients and the cooking mean booking ahead through the website is a must. **Known for:** beautifully executed traditional Roman cooking; spaghetti alla gricia (with guanciale, pecorino cheese, and black pepper); reservation list that opens 30 days at a time. ⑤ *Average main: €16* ✉ *Salita dei Crescenzi, 31, Piazza Navona* ⊕ *www.armandoalpantheon.it* ⊘ *Closed Sun. and Aug.*

★ Ba'Ghetto

$$ | **ITALIAN** | **FAMILY** | This well-established hot spot on the Jewish Ghetto's main promenade has pleasant indoor and outdoor seating. The kitchen is kosher (many places featuring Roman Jewish fare are not) and is known for its Judeo-Roman meat dishes mixed with Middle Eastern recipes. **Known for:** carciofi alla giudia (deep-fried artichokes) and other Roman-Jewish specialties; casual family atmosphere; tables on the pedestrianized street. ⑤ *Average main: €22* ✉ *Via del Portico d'Ottavia, 57, Jewish*

Ghetto ☎ 06/68892868 ⊕ www.baghetto.com ⊗ Dinner Fri. and lunch Sat. are strictly for those who observe Shabbat with advance payment.

★ Emma Pizzeria

$$$ | ROMAN | FAMILY | Smack in the middle of the city, with the freshest produce right outside its door, this pizzeria features pies made with dough by Rome's renowned family of bakers, the Rosciolis. The menu also offers a good selection of pastas, mains, and local Lazio wines. **Known for:** light, airy, and casual; thin-crust Roman pizza; tasty fritti (classic fried Roman pizzeria appetizers). ⓢ *Average main: €25* ⊠ *Via Monte della Farina, 28–29, Campo de' Fiori* ☎ *06/64760475* ⊕ *www.emmapizzeria.com.*

Il Sanlorenzo

$$$$ | SEAFOOD | A gorgeous space, with chandeliers and soaring original brickwork ceilings, is the setting for one of Rome's best seafood restaurants. Order à la carte, or if you're hungry, the eight-course tasting menu (given the quality of the fish, a relative bargain at €90), which might include cuttlefish-ink tagliatelle with mint, artichokes, and roe or shrimp from the island of Ponza with rosemary, bitter herbs, and porcini mushrooms. **Known for:** top-quality fish and seafood; spaghetti con ricci (sea urchins); elegant surroundings. ⓢ *Average main: €70* ⊠ *Via dei Chiavari, 4/5, Campo de' Fiori* ☎ *06/6865097* ⊕ *www.ilsanlorenzo.it* ⊗ *Closed 2 wks in Aug. No lunch Mon.*

★ Pierluigi

$$$$ | SEAFOOD | This chic seafood restaurant is a fun spot on balmy summer evenings, where elegant diners sip crisp white wine at tables out on the pretty Piazza de' Ricci. The carpaccio selection is exquisite, but there is also a large selection of pastas extravagantly topped with white truffles. **Known for:** top-quality fish and seafood; tables on the pretty pedestrianized piazza; elegant atmosphere with great service. ⓢ *Average main: €45* ⊠ *Piazza de' Ricci, 144, Campo de' Fiori* ☎ *06/6868717* ⊕ *www.pierluigi.it.*

★ Roscioli Salumeria con Cucina

$$ | WINE BAR | The shop in front of this wine bar will beckon you in with top-quality comestibles like hand-sliced cured ham from Italy and Spain, more than 300 cheeses, and a dizzying array of wines—but venture farther inside to try an extensive selection of unusual dishes and interesting takes on the classics. There are tables in the cozy wine cellar downstairs, but try and bag a table at the back on the ground floor (reserve well ahead; Roscioli is very popular). **Known for:** extensive wine list; arguably Rome's best spaghetti alla carbonara; unrivaled prosciutto selection.

An alimentari is a specialty food shop. Visit one to stock up on lunch or picnic fixings; some will give you samples to taste.

⑤ *Average main: €22* ✉ *Via dei Giubbonari, 21, Campo de' Fiori* ☎ *06/6875287* ⊕ *www.salumeriaroscioli.com* ⊘ *Closed 1 wk in Aug.*

☕ Coffee and Quick Bites

★ Gelateria Del Teatro
$ | **ICE CREAM** | **FAMILY** | In a window next to the entrance of this renowned gelateria, you can see the fresh fruit being used to create the day's flavors, which highlight the best of Italy—from Amalfi lemons to Alban hazelnuts. In addition to traditional options, look for interesting combinations like raspberry and sage or white chocolate with basil. **Known for:** sublime gelato; seasonal, all-natural ingredients; charming location on a cobblestone street. ⑤ *Average main: €3* ✉ *Via dei Coronari, 65/66, Piazza Navona* ☎ *06/45474880* ⊕ *www.gelateriadelteatro.it.*

★ Giolitti
$ | **ICE CREAM** | **FAMILY** | Open since 1900, Giolitti near the Pantheon is Rome's old-school gelateria par excellence. Pay in advance at the register by the door; take your receipt to the counter; and choose from dozens of flavors, including chocolate, cinnamon, and pistachio. **Known for:** excellent gelato; old-school setting; wide selection of flavors. ⑤ *Average main: €3* ✉ *Via degli Uffici del Vicario, 40, Piazza Navona* ☎ *06/6991243* ⊕ *www.giolitti.it.*

Pasticceria Boccione

$ | **BAKERY** | **FAMILY** | This tiny, old-school bakery famed for its Roman-Jewish sweet specialties is easy to spot because there is always a line snaking out the door. Service is brusque, choices are few, what's available depends on the season, and when it's sold out, it's sold out. **Known for:** ricotta and cherry tarts; pizza ebraica ("Jewish pizza," a dense baked sweet rich in nuts and raisins); no frills and no seats. ⑤ *Average main: €6* ⊠ *Via del Portico d'Ottavia, 1, Jewish Ghetto* ☎ *06/6878637* ⊙ *Closed Sat.*

Sant'Eustachio il Caffè

$ | **CAFÉ** | **FAMILY** | Frequented by tourists and government officials from the nearby Senate alike, this caffè is considered by many to make Rome's best coffee. Take it at the counter Roman-style—servers are hidden behind a huge espresso machine, where they vigorously mix the sugar and coffee to protect their secret method for the perfectly prepared cup (if you want yours without sugar here, ask for it *senza zucchero*). **Known for:** gran caffè (large sugared espresso); old-school Roman coffee bar vibe; 1930s interior. ⑤ *Average main: €3* ⊠ *Piazza Sant'Eustachio, 82, Piazza Navona* ☎ *06/68802048* ⊕ *www.caffesanteustachio.com.*

Tazza d'Oro

$ | **CAFÉ** | On the east corner of the piazza, in front of the Pantheon, this has been the place for serious coffee drinkers for nearly 80 years—there are no tables or frills, but there is a no-nonsense attitude when it comes to the dark coffee roasts that are perfect for espresso. Consider indulging in a *granita di caffè con panna* (coffee ice with whipped cream). **Known for:** coffee roasted on-site; gleaming retro interior; granita di caffè con panna. ⑤ *Average main: €3* ⊠ *Via degli Orfani, 86, Piazza Navona* ☎ *06/6789792* ⊕ *www.tazzadorocoffeeshop.com* ⊟ *No credit cards.*

Hotels

Albergo Santa Chiara

$$$$ | **HOTEL** | Guests choose this hotel, run by members of the same family for 200 years, not only for its prime location, but also its welcoming staff, top-notch service, and comfy beds. **Pros:** near the Pantheon and Santa Maria sopra Minerva; free Wi-Fi; lovely sitting area in front, overlooking the piazza. **Cons:** some rooms are on the small side; design is a bit basic given the higher price point; street-side rooms can be noisy. ⑤ *Rooms from: €310* ⊠ *Via Santa Chiara, 21, Piazza Navona* ☎ *06/6872979* ⊕ *www.albergosantachiara.com* ⇨ *96 rooms* ⓘ◎ⓘ *Free Breakfast.*

Antico Albergo del Sole al Pantheon

$$$$ | HOTEL | The granddaddy of Roman hotels and one of the oldest in the world—the doors first opened in 1467—this charming property is adjacent to the Pantheon and right in the middle of the lovely Piazza della Rotonda. **Pros:** larger rooms for groups available in an annex building; rich breakfast buffet; fabulous location. **Cons:** rooms are a bit small; complicated free Wi-Fi; not all rooms have views. ⑤ *Rooms from: €530* ✉ *Piazza della Rotonda, 63, Piazza Navona* ☎ *06/6780441* ⊕ *www.hotelsolealpantheon.com* ⇨ *27 rooms* ⦿ *Free Breakfast.*

D.O.M Hotel Roma

$$$$ | HOTEL | In an old convent on Via Giulia, one of Rome's romantic ivy-covered streets, the D.O.M (Deo Optimo Maximo) is an ultrachic luxury hotel that resembles an aristocratic *casa nobile*. **Pros:** complimentary Acqua di Parma toiletries; heated towel racks; hip decor in historic setting. **Cons:** an armed guard at the anti-terrorism headquarters opposite the hotel may be off-putting for some; delicious but expensive cocktails; standard rooms are small for a five-star hotel. ⑤ *Rooms from: €550* ✉ *Via Giulia, 131, Campo de' Fiori* ☎ *06/6832144* ⊕ *www.domhotelroma.com* ⇨ *18 rooms* ⦿ *Free Breakfast.*

G-Rough Hotel

$$$$ | HOTEL | With decor elements such as original wood-beamed ceilings, retro tiles, rich fabrics, contemporary art, and furniture that nods to 1930s and '40s Italian design, there's a hipster feel to this hotel inside a 17th-century palazzo around the corner from Piazza Navona. **Pros:** organic continental breakfast; free welcome drink at the hot-spot bar; intriguing experience packages. **Cons:** rooms facing Piazza Pasquino can be noisy; no real reception area; consciously cool decor might be too overdone for some. ⑤ *Rooms from: €550* ✉ *Piazza Pasquino, 69, Piazza Navona* ☎ *06/68801085* ⊕ *g-rough.com* ⇨ *10 rooms* ⦿ *Free Breakfast.*

Hotel Abruzzi

$$$ | HOTEL | This friendly, comfortable, family-run hotel has relatively gentle rates for such a prime location—directly in front of the Pantheon. **Pros:** magnificent Pantheon views; the piazza is a hot spot; sizable bathrooms. **Cons:** area can be somewhat noisy; breakfast is at a bar next door; elevator doesn't go to ground floor. ⑤ *Rooms from: €280* ✉ *Piazza della Rotonda, 69, Piazza Navona* ☎ *06/97841351* ⊕ *www.hotelabruzzi.it* ⇨ *26 rooms* ⦿ *Free Breakfast* Ⓜ *Spagna.*

At the center of the Jewish Ghetto you'll find Portico d'Ottavia, which was Rome's fish market in the Middle Ages.

Hotel Campo de' Fiori

$$$$ | **HOTEL** | This handsome, ivy-draped hotel is a romantic refuge in the heart of Campo de' Fiori. **Pros:** set on a gorgeous small square close to the action of the main campo; panoramic rooftop terrace; well-stocked library where one can relax and read. **Cons:** rooms are on the small side and could use updating; some apartments are too close to the area's noisy bar scene; can get pricey in high season. *Rooms from: €420 ⊠ Via del Biscione, 6, Campo de' Fiori ☎ 06/68806865 ⊕ www.hotelcampodefiori.com/en ⇨ 25 rooms ◯ Free Breakfast.*

Hotel Chapter Roma

$$$$ | **HOTEL** | The edgy, of-the-moment design at this boutique hotel juxtaposes plush mid-century Italian furnishings with street art murals and industrial touches. **Pros:** trendy design; coworking space available; lively rooftop bar in summer. **Cons:** no gym; no spa; rooms below the bar can be noisy. *Rooms from: €380 ⊠ Via di Santa Maria de' Calderari, 47, Jewish Ghetto ☎ 06/89935351 ⊕ www.chapter-roma.com ⇨ 47 rooms ◯ Free Breakfast.*

Hotel de' Ricci

$$$$ | **HOTEL** | This intimate boutique hotel from the team behind the Pierluigi restaurant is a top spot for wine lovers. **Pros:** excellent wine cellar and cigar lounge; great location on a quiet street; perks include complimentary aperitivo and priority reservations

at Pierluigi. **Cons:** there's a charge of €50 per day to bring pets; there is a weekend crowd for the brunch; no spa or gym. ⑤ *Rooms from: €680* ✉ *Via della Barchetta, 14, Campo de' Fiori* ☎ *06/6874775* ⊕ *www.hoteldericci.com* 🛏 *8 rooms* ⦿ *No Meals.*

Hotel Ponte Sisto

$$$ | HOTEL | Situated in a remodeled Renaissance palazzo with one of the prettiest patio-courtyards in Rome, this hotel is a relaxing retreat close to Campo de' Fiori and Trastevere. **Pros:** rooms with views (and some with balconies and terraces); great location between Trastevere and Campo de' Fiori; beautiful courtyard garden. **Cons:** street-side rooms can be noisy; some upgraded rooms are small and not worth the price difference; a/c is controlled centrally and requires a call to the front desk to adjust. ⑤ *Rooms from: €260* ✉ *Via dei Pettinari, 64, Campo de' Fiori* ☎ *06/6863100* ⊕ *www.hotelpontesisto.it* 🛏 *106 rooms* ⦿ *Free Breakfast.*

9 Hotel Cesàri

$$$$ | HOTEL | On a pedestrian-only street near the Pantheon, this lovely little hotel has an air of warmth and serenity, as well as a rooftop bar with great views of Rome. **Pros:** prime location; thoughtfully updated interiors; beautiful rooftop bar. **Cons:** two-night minimum; the area can be a bit noisy; rooftop bar not open in winter. ⑤ *Rooms from: €350* ✉ *Via di Pietra, 89/a, Piazza Navona* ☎ *06/6749701* ⊕ *www.9-hotel-cesari-rome.it* 🛏 *51 rooms* ⦿ *No Meals* Ⓜ *Barberini.*

The Pantheon Iconic Rome Hotel, Autograph Collection

$$$$ | HOTEL | A member of Marriott's Autograph Collection, this boutique hotel is a sleek retreat in the center of the action. **Pros:** modern design and amenities; exceptionally professional staff; Marriott Bonvoy members can redeem points. **Cons:** some rooms lack external views; no spa or gym; design might be considered a bit cold and corporate. ⑤ *Rooms from: €600* ✉ *Via di Santa Chiara, 4A, Piazza Navona* ☎ *06/87807070* ⊕ *www.thepantheonhotel.com* 🛏 *79 rooms* ⦿ *No Meals.*

Nightlife

Enoteca al Parlamento Achilli

WINE BAR | The proximity of this traditional *enoteca* (wine bar) to Montecitorio, the Italian Parliament building, makes it a favorite with journalists and politicos, who often stop in for a glass of wine after work. But it's the tantalizing smell of truffles from the snack counter, where a sommelier waits to organize your tasting, that will probably lure you inside. There's also a celebrated restaurant where you can book a table and enjoy a parade of elegant Italian plates. Don't forget to check out the wineshop, too. ✉ *Via dei Prefetti, 15, Piazza Navona* ☎ *06/6873446* ⊕ *achilli.restaurant.*

Il Goccetto
WINE BAR | Specializing in the vintages produced by smaller vineyards from Sicily to Venice, this historical wine bar also has a menu of Italian delicacies (meats and cheeses) that likewise represents the entire Italian peninsula. The burrata with sun-dried tomatoes is a perennial favorite. The tiny bar is well designed but is always busy and never accepts reservations. If all the seats are taken, you might be able to sip wine on the step outside while taking in the snippets of Roman life passing by. ✉ *Via dei Banchi Vecchi, 14, Campo de' Fiori* ☎ *06/99448583* ⊕ *www.ilgoccetto.com.*

Jerry Thomas Speakeasy
COCKTAIL BARS | One of just a handful of hidden bars in Rome, this intimate bar looks like a Prohibition-era haunt and serves the kind of classic cocktails you find in New York speakeasies. It's seating room only, so reservations must be made online in advance. Upon booking, you'll receive a password via email. Since it is a private club, the bar stays open late but patrons need to pay the €5 yearly membership fee once they arrive for the first time. Serious cocktail aficionados can also purchase specialty bitters and mixology tools at the Emporium across the alley from the drinks spot. ✉ *Vicolo Cellini, 30, Campo de' Fiori* ☎ *340/7332980 WhatsApp only* ⊕ *www.thejerrythomasproject.it.*

Shopping

★ Cartoleria Pantheon dal 1910
STATIONERY | Instead of sending a postcard home, why not send a letter written on sumptuous, handmade, Amalfi paper purchased from this shop? It also sells hand-bound leather journals in an extraordinary array of colors and sizes. There are two locations in the neighborhood. ✉ *Via della Maddalena, 41, Piazza Navona* ☎ *06/6795633* ⊕ *www.cartoleriapantheon.it.*

★ Chez Dede
SPECIALTY STORE | Husband-and-wife duo Andrea Ferolla and Daria Reina (he's a fashion illustrator, she's a photographer) curate a selection of clothes, bags, vintage jewelry, books, home decor, and anything else you might need in this cult favorite lifestyle-concept shop. Their signature fabric bags are designed to go from the plane straight to the beach club, and they regularly release

collectible items featuring Ferolla's whimsical illustrations. ✉ *Via di Monserrato, 35, Campo de' Fiori* ☎ *06/83772934* ⊕ *www.chezdede.com.*

★ L'Archivio di Monserrato

CLOTHING | Tailored jackets with exotic trims, dresses in eclectic prints and bold colors, and smart linen suits are some of the offerings at this airy, spacious boutique curated by Soledad Twombly (daughter-in-law of painter Cy Twombly). In addition to her original designs, look for a sophisticated mix of antique Turkish and Indian textiles, jewelry, shoes, and small housewares picked up on her travels. ✉ *Via di Monserrato, 150, Campo de' Fiori* ☎ *06/45654157* ⊕ *www.soledadtwombly.com.*

★ Maison Halaby

HANDBAGS | Lebanese designer and artist Gilbert Halaby was featured in fashion magazines like *Vogue* and created jewelry for Lady Gaga before giving up the rat race and opening his own shop, where the ethos is all about slow fashion. His boldly colored leather handbags incorporate suede, python, fringe, raffia, or jeweled handles, and his silk scarves are printed with his original watercolors, some of which are also on sale. The small, homey boutique—with a velvet sofa and lots of books, plants, and art by Halaby himself—is mainly open by appointment, but if you pass by, ring the bell, and if Gilbert is there, he might just invite you in for coffee or Campari. ✉ *Via di Monserrato, 21, Campo de' Fiori* ☎ *06/96521585* ⊕ *www.facebook.com/halaby.official.*

Massimo Maria Melis

JEWELRY & WATCHES | Drawing heavily on ancient Roman and Etruscan designs, the jewelry from former costume designer Massimo Maria Melis will carry you back in time. Working with 21-carat gold, he often incorporates antique coins in many of his exquisite bracelets and necklaces. Some of his pieces are done with an ancient technique, much loved by the Etruscans, in which tiny gold droplets are fused together to create intricately patterned designs. ✉ *Via dell'Orso, 57, Piazza Navona* ☎ *06/6869188* ⊕ *www.massimomariamelis.com.*

Chapter 6

TREVI AND PIAZZA DI SPAGNA

Updated by
Laura Itzkowitz

👁 Sights	🍴 Restaurants	🛏 Hotels	🛍 Shopping	🍷 Nightlife
★★★★★	★★★★★	★★★★★	★☆☆☆☆	★☆☆☆☆

Trevi and Piazza di Spagna Walking Tour

Some of Rome's grandest monuments and fountains populate this area, which has been drawing well-heeled travelers since the days of the Roman Empire and was a magnet for English artists and writers on the Grand Tour.

1 Begin your walk at the Trevi Fountain, one of Rome's most famous landmarks. The fountain is truly monumental in scale, with a larger-than-life sculpture of Oceanus surrounded by sea beasts, mermaids, and seashells spouting water in a theatrical display of 18th-century Baroque art and engineering. (The water is pumped in via the Acqua Vergine aqueduct created by Agrippa in 18 BC.) Legend has it that if you throw a coin into the fountain with your right hand over your left shoulder, you'll return to Rome; toss two coins and you'll return and fall in love; three and you'll return, find love, and marry.

2 After you've had your photo opportunity at the fountain, walk west toward Via del Tritone, one of the city's main arteries. The street connects Via del Corso with Piazza Barberini, where you can admire another spectacular fountain by Bernini.

Walking Tour 101

HIGHLIGHTS
Trevi Fountain, the Spanish Steps, Fontana della Barcaccia, Antico Caffè Greco

WHERE TO START
Trevi Fountain

LENGTH
1-2 hours, depending on your pace and how often you stop

WHERE TO END
Monument to Victor Emanuele II

BEST TIME TO GO
Early in the morning if you want to avoid the crowds

WORST TIME TO GO
On a rainy day

125

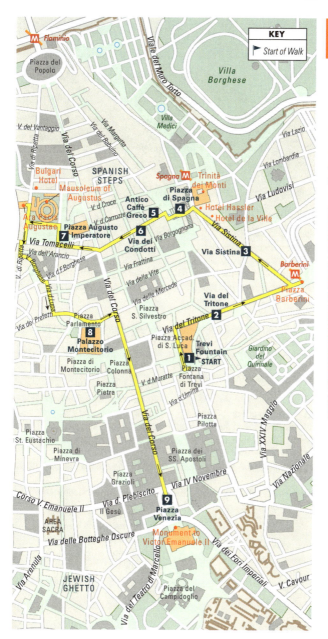

6

Trevi and Piazza di Spagna

TREVI AND PIAZZA DI SPAGNA WALKING TOUR

The Spanish steps link the Piazza di Spagna to Piazza Trinità dei Monti.

3 Walk uphill, but just before you reach Piazza Barberini, turn left onto Via Sistina, a picturesque, sloping street. As you stroll toward the Spanish Steps, you'll pass upscale boutiques and luxury hotels like Hotel de la Ville and the Hassler, which both draw celebrities and other VIP guests.

4 When you arrive at Piazza di Spagna, you'll be at the top of the Spanish Steps. Take a moment to admire the view before you descend the steps, which were built in 1723 and named for the Spanish Embassy to the Vatican on the piazza. At the bottom, you can get the best photos of the steps and the Trinità dei Monti church with Bernini's Barcaccia fountain in the foreground.

5 You might want to stop for a cappuccino at Antico Caffè Greco, Rome's oldest caffè. Having been frequented by Byron, Shelley, Keats, and Goethe, its wood-lined walls and ornate furnishings are steeped in history.

6 Stroll west on Via dei Condotti, Rome's most upscale shopping street, passing by designer stores like Prada and Dolce & Gabbana. In a few minutes, you'll reach Via del Corso. When Via dei Condotti meets Via del Corso, take the fork on the right and follow Via Tomacelli.

7 After a couple more blocks, you'll reach Piazza Augusto Imperatore, where you can see exactly how the ancient and the modern form the backdrop of everyday life in the Eternal

City. In the middle of the square is the Mausoleum of Augustus, the world's largest circular tomb, which the emperor commissioned when he was just 35. Surrounding it to the north and east are Rationalist buildings built during Mussolini's reign, one of which now houses the swanky Bulgari Hotel. To the west is the Ara Pacis Augustae, a stark white museum built by Richard Meier to house the ancient altar built to celebrate the Pax Romana, a period of peace following Augustus' military victories. You might want to make a quick stop to visit the museum and see the altar up close; the downstairs galleries house rotating exhibitions.

8 After you've seen the Ara Pacis, start walking south on Via di Ripetta, then turn left onto Via Borghese, continue on Via della Lupaia, and turn left again on Via dei Prefetti. You'll pass by Palazzo Montecitorio, the Chamber of Deputies, before turning right onto Via del Corso.

The Ara Pacis Augustae

9 Walk for a little more than half a mile to get to Piazza Venezia, the massive square where you can see the Monument to Victor Emanuele II, also known as the Vittoriano. Built to honor Italy's unification and the country's first king, it also shelters the eternal flame at the tomb of the unknown soldier. For panoramic views of the city, pay the €10 ticket to take the elevator up to the rooftop terrace.

NEIGHBORHOOD SNAPSHOT

TOP EXPERIENCES

■ **Trevi Fountain:** Iconic would be an understatement for this Elvis of waterworks—overblown, flashy, and reliably thronged by legions of fans. Throw in a coin and guarantee a return to the Eternal City.

■ **The Spanish Steps:** Saunter seductively up (but don't sit on) the world's most celebrated stairway.

■ **The Ceiling of San Ignazio:** Stand beneath the stupendous ceiling of Rome's most splendiferous Baroque church, and, courtesy of painter-priest Fra Andrea Pozzo, be transported heavenward.

■ **Monumento a Vittorio Emanuele II:** Admire the enormous marble monument built in honor of the first king of unified Italy.

■ **Fabulous palazzi:** Visit the ornate Palazzo Doria Pamphilj and the Palazzo Colonna for an intimate look at the homes of Rome's 17th-century aristocrats, brimming with priceless artworks.

■ **Shopping:** On Via dei Condotti and Via del Babuino, you can flit effortlessly from Bulgari to Gucci to Valentino to Ferragamo. But save your shopping muscles for Roman boutiques that you can't find anywhere else.

GETTING HERE

■ Piazza di Spagna is a short 10- to 15-minute walk from Piazza del Popolo, the Pantheon, and Villa Borghese. One of Rome's handiest subway stations, Spagna (Metro A), is tucked just left of the steps. Barberini (Metro A) is a 10-minute walk away. Bus No. 119 (from Piazza del Popolo and Piazza Venezia) passes above, stopping at Piazza Trinità dei Monti.

■ The Trevi Fountain is about a 10-minute walk south from Piazza di Spagna, along the bustling Via del Corso.

In both spirit and in fact, this area is grandiose. The overblown Vittoriano monument, the labyrinthine palaces of Rome's surviving aristocracy, and the diamond-studded denizens of Via Condotti all embody the exuberant ego of a city at the center of its own universe. Here's where you'll see ladies in fur as you walk through a thousand snapshots while climbing the famous Spanish Steps.

6

Trevi and Piazza di Spagna

If Rome has a Main Street, it's Via del Corso, which is often jammed with Roman teenagers, in from the city's outlying districts for a ritual stroll that resembles a strutting promenade of peacocks in blue jeans. Along this thoroughfare it's easy to forget that the gray and stolid atmosphere comes partially from the enormous palaces lining both sides of the street. Many were built over the past 300 years by princely families who wanted to secure front-row seats for the frantic antics of Carnevale, which once sent horses racing down the street from Piazza del Popolo to Piazza Venezia. Beyond the prim entrances of these structures, however, are some of Rome's grandest 17th- and 18th-century treasures, including ornate golden ballrooms and Old Master paintings.

◉ Sights

★ **Ara Pacis Augustae** (*Altar of Augustan Peace*)
MONUMENT | This pristine monument sits inside one of Rome's contemporary architectural landmarks: a gleaming, rectangular, glass-and-travertine structure designed by American architect Richard Meier. It overlooks the Tiber on one side and the ruins of the marble-clad Mausoleo di Augusto (Mausoleum of Augustus) on the other and is a serene, luminous oasis right in the center of Rome.

This altar itself dates from 13 BC and was commissioned to celebrate the Pax Romana, the era of peace ushered in by Augustus's military victories. When viewing it, keep in mind that the spectacular reliefs would have been painted in vibrant colors, now long

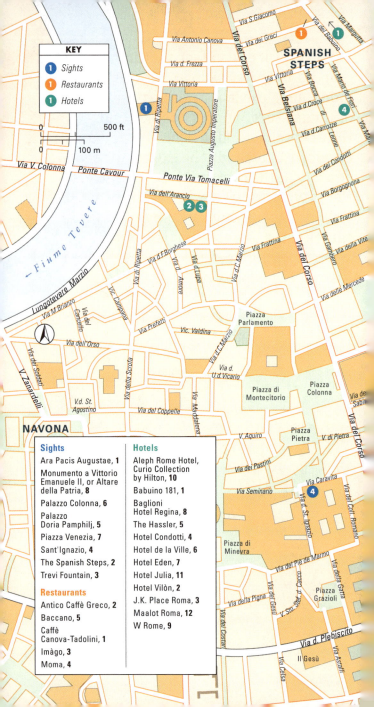

gone. The reliefs on the short sides portray myths associated with Rome's founding and glory; those on the long sides display a procession of the imperial family. Although half of his body is missing, Augustus is identifiable as the first full figure at the procession's head on the south-side frieze; academics still argue over exact identifications of most of the figures. Be sure to check out the small downstairs museum, which hosts rotating exhibits on Italian culture, with themes ranging from design to film. ✉ *Lungotevere in Augusta, at the corner of Via Tomacelli, Piazza di Spagna* ☎ *06/0608* ⊕ *www.arapacis.it* 🎟 *€12, €13 when there is an exhibition* ♿ *Reservations essential for groups of 11 to 25 persons* Ⓜ *Flaminio.*

★ Monumento a Vittorio Emanuele II, or Altare della Patria (*Victor Emmanuel II Monument, or Altar of the Nation*)

MONUMENT | The huge white mass known as the "Vittoriano" is an inescapable landmark that has been likened to a giant wedding cake or an immense typewriter. Present-day Romans joke that you can only avoid looking at it if you are standing on it, but at the beginning of the 20th century, it was the source of great civic pride. Built to honor the unification of Italy and the nation's first king, Victor Emmanuel II, it also shelters the eternal flame at the tomb of Italy's Unknown Soldier, killed during World War I. Alas, to create this elaborate marble behemoth and the vast surrounding piazza, its architects blithely destroyed many ancient and medieval buildings and altered the slope of the Campidoglio (Capitoline Hill), which abuts it.

The underwhelming exhibit inside the building tells the history of the country's unification. The Vittoriano has a rooftop terrace, however, that offers the best panoramic views of Rome. ✉ *Entrances on Piazza Venezia, Piazza del Campidoglio, and Via di San Pietro in Carcere, Trevi* ☎ *06/0608* ⊕ *vive.cultura.gov.it* 🎟 *Main building free; €17 for the terrace* Ⓜ *Colosseo.*

★ Palazzo Colonna

CASTLE/PALACE | Rome's grandest private palace is a fusion of 17th- and 18th-century buildings that have been occupied by the Colonna family for more than 20 generations. The immense residence faces Piazza dei Santi Apostoli on one side and the Quirinale (Quirinal Hill) on the other—with a little bridge over Via della Pilotta linking to gardens on the hill—and contains an art gallery that's open to the public on Saturday morning or by guided tour on Friday morning.

The gallery is itself a setting of aristocratic grandeur; you might recognize the Sala Grande as the site where Audrey Hepburn meets the press in *Roman Holiday*. An ancient red marble *colonna* (column), which is the family's emblem, looms at one end, but the most spectacular feature is the ceiling fresco of the Battle of Lepanto painted by Giovanni Coli and Filippo Gherardi beginning in 1675. Adding to the opulence are works by Poussin, Tintoretto, and Veronese, as well as portraits of illustrious members of the family, such as Vittoria Colonna, Michelangelo's muse and longtime friend.

It's worth paying an extra fee to take the guided, English-language gallery tour, which will help you navigate through the array of madonnas, saints, goddesses, popes, and cardinals to see Annibale Carracci's lonely *Beaneater*, spoon at the ready and front teeth missing. The gallery also has a caffè with a pleasant terrace. ✉ *Via della Pilotta, 17, Trevi* ☎ *06/6784350* ⊕ *www.galleriacolonna. it* ⌨ *€15 for gallery and gardens, €25 to also visit the Princess Isabelle Apartment, €30 for a guided tour on Friday* ⊙ *Closed Sun.–Thurs.* ☞ *Friday for guided tour only* Ⓜ *Barberini.*

★ Palazzo Doria Pamphilj

CASTLE/PALACE | Like the Palazzo Colonna and the Galleria Borghese, this dazzling 15th-century palace provides a fantastic glimpse of aristocratic Rome. It passed through several hands before becoming the property of the Pamphilj family, who married into the famous seafaring Doria family of Genoa in the 18th century. The family still lives in part of the palace.

The understated beauty of the graceful facade, designed by Gabriele Valvassori in 1730 and best admired from the opposite side of the street, barely hints at the interior's opulent halls and gilded galleries, which are filled with Old Master works. The 550 paintings here include three by Caravaggio: *St. John the Baptist, Mary Magdalene,* and the breathtaking *Rest on the Flight to Egypt.* Off the eye-popping Galleria degli Specchi (Gallery of Mirrors)—a smaller version of the one at Versailles—are the famous Velázquez *Pope Innocent X,* considered by some historians to be the greatest portrait ever painted, and the Bernini bust of the same Pamphilj pope.

A delightful audio guide is included in the ticket price and is narrated by the current heir, Prince Jonathan Doria Pamphilj, who divulges intimate family history. Plan to stay for lunch, or at least pause for a coffee, at the fashionable Caffè Doria, with elegant tables set out in the palace's peaceful cloisters. ✉ *Via del Corso, 305, Trevi* ☎ *06/6797323* ⊕ *www.doriapamphilj.it* ⌨ *€16* ⊙ *Closed the 3rd Wed. of the month* ⌨ *Reservations required* Ⓜ *Barberini.*

Piazza Venezia

PLAZA/SQUARE | Piazza Venezia stands at what was the beginning of the ancient Via Flaminia, a historic Roman road leading northeast across Italy to the Adriatic Sea. From this square, Rome's geographic heart, all distances from the city are calculated.

The piazza was transformed at the turn of the 20th century when much older ruins were destroyed to make way for a modern capital city (and a massive monument to unified Italy's first king). The female bust near the church of San Marco in the southwest corner of the piazza is a fragment of a statue of Isis, now known to the Romans as Madama Lucrezia. It is one of the city's "talking statues" on which anonymous poets hung verses pungent with political satire.

The Via Flaminia remains a vital artery. The part leading from Piazza Venezia to Piazza del Popolo is now known as Via del Corso, after the horse races (*corse*) that were run here during the wild Roman carnival celebrations of the 17th and 18th centuries. It also happens to be one of Rome's busiest shopping streets. ✉ *Piazza Venezia, Trevi*.

★ Sant'Ignazio

CHURCH | Rome's second Jesuit church, this 17th-century landmark set on a Rococo piazza harbors some of the city's most magnificent trompe l'oeils. To get the full effect of the illusionistic ceiling by priest-artist Andrea Pozzo, stand on the small yellow disk set into the floor of the nave. The heavenly vision that seems to extend upward almost indefinitely represents the *Allegory of the Missionary Work of the Jesuits*. It's part of Pozzo's cycle of works in this church exalting the early history of the Jesuit order, whose founder was the reformer Ignatius of Loyola. The saint soars heavenward, supported by a cast of thousands, creating a jaw-dropping effect that was fully intended to rival that of the glorious ceiling by Baciccia in the nearby mother church of Il Gesù. Be sure to have coins handy for the machine that switches on the lights so you can marvel at the false dome, which is actually a flat canvas—a trompe l'oeil trick Pozzo used when the architectural budget drained dry.

Scattered around the nave are several awe-inspiring altars; their soaring columns, gold-on-gold decoration, and gilded statues are pure splendor. Splendid, too, are the occasional sacred music concerts performed by choirs from all over the world. Look for posters by the main doors, or check the website for more information. ✉ *Piazza S. Ignazio, Trevi* ✥ *Via del Caravita 8A* ☎ *06/6794406* ⊕ *santignazio.gesuiti.it*.

★ The Spanish Steps

OTHER ATTRACTION | FAMILY | The iconic Spanish Steps (often called simply *la scalinata,* or "the staircase," by Italians) and the Piazza di Spagna from which they ascend both get their names from the Spanish Embassy to the Vatican on the piazza—even though the staircase was built with French funds by an Italian in 1723. In honor of a diplomatic visit by the King of Spain, the hillside was transformed by architect Francesco de Sanctis with a spectacular piece of urban planning to link the church of Trinità dei Monti at the top with the Via Condotti below.

In an allusion to the church, the staircase is divided by three landings (beautifully lined with potted azaleas from mid-April to mid-May). Bookending the bottom of the steps are beloved holdovers from the 18th century, when the area was known as the "English Ghetto": to the right, the Keats-Shelley House and to the left, Babington's Tea Rooms—both beautifully redolent of the era of the Grand Tour.

For weary sightseers who find the 135 steps too daunting, there is an elevator at Vicolo del Bottino 8, next to the Metro entrance. (Those with mobility problems should be aware that there is still a small flight of stairs after, however, and that the elevator is sporadically closed for repair.) At the bottom of the steps, Pietro Bernini's splendid 17th-century Barcaccia Fountain still spouts drinking water from the ancient aqueduct known as the Aqua Vergine. ✉ *Piazza di Spagna, Piazza di Spagna* Ⓜ *Spagna.*

★ Trevi Fountain

FOUNTAIN | FAMILY | Alive with rushing waters commanded by an imperious sculpture of Oceanus, the Fontana di Trevi has been all about theatrical effects from the start; it is an aquatic marvel in a city filled with them. The fountain's unique drama is largely due to its location: its vast basin is squeezed into the tight confluence of three little streets (the *tre vie,* which may give the fountain its name), with cascades emerging as if from the wall of Palazzo Poli.

The dream of a fountain emerging full force from a palace was first envisioned by Bernini and Pietro da Cortona from Pope Urban VIII's plan to rebuild an older fountain, which had earlier marked the end point of the Acqua Vergine, an aqueduct created in 18 BC by Agrippa. Three popes later, under Pope Clement XIII, Nicola Salvi finally broke ground with his winning design. Unfortunately, Salvi did not live to see his masterpiece of sculpted seashells, roaring sea beasts, and diva-like mermaids completed; he caught a cold and died while working in the culverts of the aqueduct 11 years before the fountain was finished in 1762.

Everyone knows the famous legend that if you throw a coin into the Trevi Fountain you will ensure a return trip to the Eternal City, but not everyone knows how to do it the right way. You must toss a coin with your right hand over your left shoulder, with your back to the fountain. One coin means you'll return to Rome; two, you'll return *and* fall in love; three, you'll return, find love, and marry. The fountain grosses some €600,000 a year, with every cent going to the Italian Red Cross, which is why Fendi was willing to fully fund the Trevi's recent restoration.

Tucked away in a little nearby alley is the Vicus Caprarius (✉ *Vicolo del Puttarello, 25*), a small museum where visitors can pay €8 for a guided tour that descends into a subterranean area that gives a glimpse at the water source that keeps the fountain running. ✉ *Piazza di Trevi, Trevi* Ⓜ *Barberini*.

🍴 Restaurants

Antico Caffè Greco

$ | **CAFÉ** | The red-velvet chairs and marble tables of one of Rome's oldest caffès have seen the likes of Byron, Shelley, Keats, Goethe, and Casanova. Locals love basking in the more than 260 years of history held within its dark-wood walls lined with antique artwork; tourists appreciate its location amid the shopping madness of upscale Via Condotti. **Known for:** lavish historic design; perfect espresso; crystal goblets and high prices to match. 💲 *Average main: €12* ✉ *Via dei Condotti, 86, Piazza di Spagna* ☎ *06/6791700* ⊕ *anticocaffegreco.eu* Ⓜ *Spagna*.

Baccano

$$$ | **BRASSERIE** | There are plenty of options for good food at reasonable prices around the Trevi Fountain, but this Paris-inspired brasserie—open for lunch, dinner, and everything in between—is a great bet. Although it emphasizes seafood, the extensive menu has something for everyone, from salads to pasta and entrées. **Known for:** oyster bar; excellent carbonara; classic international cocktails. 💲 *Average main: €28* ✉ *Via delle Muratte, 23, Trevi* ☎ *06/69941166* ⊕ *www.baccanoroma.com* Ⓜ *Barberini*.

Caffè Canova-Tadolini

$ | **CAFÉ** | On chic Via del Babuino, the former studio of Neoclassical sculptor Antonio Canova and his student, Adamo Tadolini, is now an atmospheric spot for coffee, snack, or lunch. Opt for the budget-friendly option of taking your coffee at the bar while admiring the enormous plaster copies of the maestros' work, or pay more for table service and sit amid vast sculptures. **Known for:** museum-like setting; respectable aperitivo snacks for the price;

slow and serious service. $ *Average main: €5* ⊠ *Via del Babuino, 150/A, Piazza di Spagna* ☎ *06/32110702* ⊕ *www.canovatadolini. com* Ⓜ *Spagna*.

Imàgo
$$$$ | **MODERN ITALIAN** | Excellence is at the forefront of everything at Imàgo, the Michelin-starred restaurant inside the legendary Hotel Hassler, now headed by young star chef Andrea Antonini. You can order à la carte, but this is the place to splurge on a tasting menu. **Known for:** tempting tasting menus; innovative creations inspired by all of Italy; sweeping city views from rooftop terrace. $ *Average main: €50* ⊠ *Hotel Hassler, Piazza Trinità dei Monti, 6, Piazza di Spagna* ☎ *06/69934726* ⊕ *www.hotelhasslerroma.com* ⊗ *Closed Sun. and Mon. No lunch* Ⓜ *Spagna*.

★ Moma
$$$ | **MODERN ITALIAN** | In front of the American embassy and a favorite of the design *trendoisie*, Michelin-starred Moma attracts well-heeled businessmen at lunch but turns into a more intimate affair for dinner. The kitchen turns out hits as it creates *alta cucina* (haute cuisine) made using Italian ingredients sourced from small producers. **Known for:** pasta with a twist; creative presentation; affordable fine dining. $ *Average main: €25* ⊠ *Via San Basilio, 42, Piazza di Spagna* ☎ *06/42011798* ⊕ *www.ristorantemoma.it* ⊗ *Closed Sun. No lunch Sat.* Ⓜ *Barberini*.

Hotels

Aleph Rome Hotel, Curio Collection by Hilton
$$$$ | **HOTEL** | Fashionable couples tend to favor the Aleph, a former bank–turned–luxury hotel, where the motto seems to be "more marble, everywhere." The abundant facilities include two pools (one in the spa and one on the roof), a cigar lounge, a cocktail bar, and two restaurants (one on the ground floor and one on the rooftop). **Pros:** free access to the spa for hotel guests; award-winning design; terrace with small pool. **Cons:** rooms are petite for the price; rooftop views don't showcase Rome's most flattering side; buffet breakfast not included. $ *Rooms from: €448* ⊠ *Via San Basilio, 15, Piazza di Spagna* ☎ *06/4229001* ⊕ *alephrome.com* ⇌ *80 rooms and suites* ⊗ *No Meals* Ⓜ *Barberini*.

Babuino 181
$$$ | **HOTEL** | On chic Via del Babuino, known for its high-end boutiques, jewelry stores, and antiques shops, this discreet and stylish hotel is an ideal pied-à-terre, with spacious rooms spread over two historic buildings. **Pros:** spacious suites; luxury Frette

Did You Know?

The 15th-century Palazzo Doria Pamphilj provides a dazzling glimpse of aristocratic Rome, especially in its Galleria degli Specchi (Gallery of Mirrors)—a smaller version of the one at Versailles.

linens; iPhone docks and other handy in-room amenities. **Cons:** rooms can be a bit noisy; breakfast is nothing special; annex rooms feel removed from service staff. ⑤ *Rooms from: €261* ✉ *Via del Babuino, 181, Piazza di Spagna* ☎ *06/32295295* ⊕ *www.romeluxurysuites.com/it/babuino-181* ⇌ *25 rooms* ⦿ *Free Breakfast* Ⓜ *Flaminio, Spagna.*

Baglioni Hotel Regina

$$$$ | HOTEL | The former home of Queen Margherita of Savoy, the Baglioni Hotel Regina, which enjoys a prime spot on the Via Veneto, is still a favorite among today's jet-setters. **Pros:** chic decor; luxury on-site spa; excellent on-site restaurant and bar. **Cons:** internal rooms overlook air-conditioning ducts; extra charge for breakfast à la carte; location isn't as prestigious as it once was. ⑤ *Rooms from: €650* ✉ *Via Veneto, 72, Piazza di Spagna* ☎ *06/421111* ⊕ *www.baglionihotels.com/rome* ⇌ *117 rooms* ⦿ *No Meals* Ⓜ *Barberini.*

★ The Hassler

$$$$ | HOTEL | When it comes to million-dollar views, the best place to stay in the whole city is the Hassler, so it's no surprise many of the rich and famous (Tom Cruise, Jennifer Lopez, and the Beckhams among them) are willing to pay top dollar for a room at this exclusive hotel atop the Spanish Steps. **Pros:** prime location and panoramic views; exceptional service; sauna access included with each reservation. **Cons:** VIP rates (10% VAT not included); gym and wellness area is tiny; rooms are updated on a rolling basis, leaving some feeling dated. ⑤ *Rooms from: €1,400* ✉ *Piazza Trinità dei Monti, 6, Piazza di Spagna* ☎ *06/699340, 800/223–6800 in U.S.* ⊕ *www.hotelhasslerroma.com* ⇌ *87 rooms and suites* ⦿ *Free Breakfast* Ⓜ *Spagna.*

Hotel Condotti

$$ | B&B/INN | Near the most expensive shopping street in Rome, Via Condotti, and one block from the Spanish Steps, this delightful little hotel is all about peace, comfort, and location. **Pros:** soundproof rooms with terraces; individual climate control; gorgeous decor. **Cons:** small rooms; tiny elevator; annex rooms on a different street without front desk support. ⑤ *Rooms from: €140* ✉ *Via Mario de' Fiori, 37, Piazza di Spagna* ☎ *06/6794661* ⊕ *www.hotelcondotti.com* ⇌ *87 rooms* ⦿ *Free Breakfast* Ⓜ *Spagna.*

★ Hotel de la Ville

$$$$ | HOTEL | Occupying a prime position atop the Spanish Steps, this glamorous sister property of the beloved Hotel de Russie near the Piazza del Popolo has as a Grand Tour–inspired design featuring antiques, custom wallpaper stamped with Piranesi

A sculptural masterpiece from the Baroque era, the Trevi Fountain is also a cultural icon, appearing in countless works of art, literature, and movies.

prints, and plenty of silk. **Pros:** must-visit rooftop bar with panoramic views; prestigious location atop the Spanish Steps; pampering spa uses signature made-in-Italy organic products. **Cons:** some rooms are a bit small for the price; service can be a bit slow at the bar; no pets allowed. ⑤ *Rooms from: €1,400* ✉ *Via Sistina, 69, Piazza di Spagna* ☎ *06/977931* ⊕ *www.roccofortehotels.com* ⇌ *104 rooms and suites* ⎟⚬⎢ *Free Breakfast* Ⓜ *Spagna.*

★ Hotel Eden

$$$$ | **HOTEL** | At what was once a favorite haunt of Ingrid Bergman, Ginger Rogers, and Fellini, dashing elegance, exquisite decor, and stunning vistas of Rome combine with true Italian hospitality. **Pros:** gorgeous rooftop terrace restaurant; tranquil spa facilities; 24-hour room service. **Cons:** breakfast not included (and very expensive, at €50); gym is standard but small; some rooms overlook an unremarkable courtyard. ⑤ *Rooms from: €1,260* ✉ *Via Ludovisi, 49, Piazza di Spagna* ☎ *06/478121* ⊕ *www.dorchestercollection. com/en/rome/hotel-eden* ⇌ *98 rooms and suites* ⎟⚬⎢ *No Meals* Ⓜ *Spagna.*

Hotel Julia

$$$ | **HOTEL** | This small hotel, situated on a small cobblestone street just behind Piazza Barberini and a short walk to the Trevi Fountain, offers relatively spacious rooms that won't break the bank. **Pros:** safe neighborhood; convenient to sights and transportation; moderate prices for a central area. **Cons:** some street noise at night; very basic accommodations; some rooms are

dark and cramped. ⑤ *Rooms from: €300* ✉ *Via Rasella, 29, Trevi* ☎ *06/83652440* ⊕ *www.hotelјulia.it* ⇌ *30 rooms* ⦿ *Free Breakfast* Ⓜ *Barberini*.

★ Hotel Vilòn

$$$$ | **HOTEL** | Set in a 16th-century mansion annexed to Palazzo Borghese and tucked behind a discreet entrance, this intimate hotel might be Rome's best-kept secret. **Pros:** gorgeous design; attentive staff; fantastic location. **Cons:** no spa or gym; not much communal space; some rooms are a bit small. ⑤ *Rooms from: €780* ✉ *Via dell'Arancio, 69, Piazza di Spagna* ☎ *06/878187* ⊕ *www.hotelvilon.com* ⇌ *18 rooms and suites* ⦿ *Free Breakfast* Ⓜ *Spagna*.

J.K. Place Roma

$$$$ | **HOTEL** | Set in what was once an architecture school and featuring gorgeous modern design, this intimate hotel is a stone's throw from the Mausoleum of Augustus and not far from the Spanish Steps and Piazza del Popolo. **Pros:** stellar staff are eager to please; excellent meals at rooftop lounge; complimentary minibar. **Cons:** no fitness center; not all rooms have a balcony; some rooms are on the small side. ⑤ *Rooms from: €800* ✉ *Via Monte d'Oro, 30, Piazza di Spagna* ☎ *06/982634* ⊕ *jkroma.com* ⇌ *27 rooms and suites* ⦿ *Free Breakfast* Ⓜ *Spagna*.

Maalot Roma

$$$$ | **HOTEL** | This boutique property inside the former residence of opera composer Gaetano Donizetto aims to be a restaurant with rooms above rather than a hotel with a restaurant below. **Pros:** chic design with original art; great food at Don Pasquale restaurant; central location just steps from the Trevi Fountain. **Cons:** some rooms look directly onto the McDonald's across the street; no spa; service can be a bit slow. ⑤ *Rooms from: €750* ✉ *Via delle Murate, 78, Trevi* ☎ *06/878087* ⊕ *www.hotelmaalot.com* ⇌ *30 rooms and suites* ⦿ *Free Breakfast* Ⓜ *Barberini*.

W Rome

$$$$ | **HOTEL** | On a quiet street between Via Veneto and the Spanish Steps, the W Rome brings a calculated cool to an upscale old-world area. **Pros:** craft cocktails; rooftop pool and lounge area; live music and a popular brunch add to the buzz. **Cons:** no spa; live music can be a pain; 24/7 energy not for everyone. ⑤ *Rooms from: €549* ✉ *Via Liguria, 26–36, Piazza di Spagna* ☎ *06/894121* ⊕ *www.marriott.com* ⇌ *162 rooms and suites* ⦿ *Free Breakfast* Ⓜ *Barberini*.

Nightlife

Antica Enoteca
WINE BAR | Piazza di Spagna's historic wine bar literally corners the market on prime people-watching. Cozy up to the counter to sip a drink under the charming frescoes, or snag a coveted outdoor table. In addition to a vast selection of wine, Antica Enoteca has delectable antipasti, perfect for a snack or a light lunch, as well as a full menu of pastas and pizzas. ✉ *Via della Croce, 76/b, Piazza di Spagna* ☎ *06/6790896* ⊕ *www.anticaenoteca.com* Ⓜ *Spagna.*

Il Marchese
COCKTAIL BARS | With high bar stools and midnight blue accents, Il Marchese feels every bit the sophisticated Roman nightcap hot spot. It was the first amaro bar in Europe, stocking more than 500 labels of the bitter, herbal liqueur, which can be served straight or mixed into creative cocktails. Pop in for a tapas-style aperitivo, or stay for dinner and watch the chef "shop" from his market of gourmet Italian ingredients that takes up part of the space. ✉ *Via di Ripetta, 162, Piazza di Spagna* ☎ *06/90218872* ⊕ *www.ilmarcheseroma.it* Ⓜ *Spagna.*

Il Palazzetto Wine Bar
WINE BAR | This rooftop wine bar and restaurant wins the prize for the perfect aperitivo spot, with excellent drinks and appetizers, as well as a breathtaking view of the comings and goings on the Spanish Steps. Reach it by climbing the monumental staircase that it overlooks, or getting a lift from the elevator inside the Spagna Metro station. ✉ *Il Palazzetto, Vicolo del Bottino, 8, Piazza di Spagna* ✣ *The main entrance is a small gate at the top of the Spanish Steps* ☎ *342/1507215* ⊕ *www.hotelhasslerroma.com/en/il-palazzetto* Ⓜ *Spagna.*

Shopping

Ex Libris
BOOKS | Founded in 1931, one of Rome's oldest and largest antiquarian bookshops has a distinctive selection of scholarly and collectible books from the 16th to 20th century. In addition to rare and early editions on art and architecture, music and theater, and literature and humanities, the shop sells maps and prints. ✉ *Via dell' Umiltà, 77/a, Trevi* ☎ *06/6791540* ⊕ *www.exlibrisroma.it* Ⓜ *Barberini.*

Galleria Alberto Sordi
MALL | This gorgeous covered shopping arcade on the Piazza Colonna was envisioned in the late 19th century, but not opened to the public until 1922. A Neoclassical palazzo with a brilliant stained-glass ceiling, the indoor mall is home to individual boutiques with both big and small names. ✉ *Piazza Colonna, Piazza di Spagna* ⊕ *galleriaalbertosordi.com* Ⓜ *Barberini.*

★ La Rinascente
DEPARTMENT STORE | **FAMILY** | Set in a dazzling, seven-story space, Italy's best-known department store is packed topped to bottom with luxury goods, from cosmetics, handbags, and accessories to ready-to-wear designer sportswear to kitchen items and housewares. Even if you're not planning on buying anything, the basement excavations of a Roman aqueduct and the roof terrace bar with its splendid view are well worth a visit. There's also a location at Piazza Fiume. ✉ *Via del Tritone, 61, Piazza di Spagna* ☏ *02/91387388* ⊕ *www.rinascente.it* Ⓜ *Barberini.*

★ Pineider
STATIONERY | This outfit has been making exclusive stationery since 1774. The first Rome shop opened at the request of the royal household, and this is where the city's aristocratic families still come for engraved wedding invitations and timeless visiting cards. It also sells desk accessories, wallets, and briefcases made using the best Florentine leather. ✉ *Via del Leoncino, 25, Piazza di Spagna* ☏ *06/6795884* ⊕ *www.pineider.com* Ⓜ *Spagna.*

Schostal
CLOTHING | A Piazza di Spagna fixture since 1870, this was once the go-to shop for corsets, petticoats, stockings, and bonnets. Today, it's the place to stop for essential basics that are increasingly difficult to find, like fine-quality shirts, underwear, and handkerchiefs made of wool and pure cashmere at affordable prices. ✉ *Via della Fontanella di Borghese, 29, Piazza di Spagna* ☏ *06/6791240* ⊕ *www.schostaloriginals.com* Ⓜ *Spagna.*

Superga
SHOES | In business for more than 100 years and beloved by many Italians, Superga sells timeless sneakers in classic white or a rainbow of colors. The 2750 model has been worn by everyone from Kelly Brook to the Princess of Wales. There is another location on Via di Campo Marzio. ✉ *Via delle Vite, 86, Piazza di Spagna* ☏ *06/6787654* ⊕ *www.superga.com* Ⓜ *Spagna.*

Chapter 7

VILLA BORGHESE AND ENVIRONS

Updated by
Laura Itzkowitz

Sights	Restaurants	Hotels	Shopping	Nightlife
★★★★☆	★★☆☆☆	★★★☆☆	★☆☆☆☆	★☆☆☆☆

Villa Borghese and Environs Walking Tour

Rome's green lung is the leafy Villa Borghese park, which extends from Piazza del Popolo to Parioli, with museums, a lake, and more in between. Piazza del Popolo was the northern gateway to Rome and is still one of the city's most impressive squares.

1 **Begin this tour after spending an hour or two visiting Galleria Borghese,** the museum that houses masterpieces of Baroque art by Bernini and Caravaggio, which is located in the northeastern part of the park. (Be sure to book timed tickets in advance if you want to visit the museum.) The entire park was once part of the estate of the wealthy and powerful Borghese family.

2 **With the museum behind you, begin your leisurely stroll heading southwest on Viale del Museo Borghese.** Follow the paved roads or venture off onto the dirt paths. The Pincio Promenade is about a mile from the museum, so it should take between 20 and 30 minutes to get there, depending on your pace and how often you stop. On the way there, you can admire the Fountain of the Seahorses; the Piazza di Siena, which hosts open-air concerts and equestrian events; the

Walking Tour 101

HIGHLIGHTS
Galleria Borghese, Villa Borghese, Pincio Promenade, Piazza del Popolo, Canova, Via Margutta, Il Marmoraro

WHERE TO START
Galleria Borghese

LENGTH
1–2 hours, depending on your pace and how many stops you make

WHERE TO END
Via Margutta

BEST TIME TO GO
Late afternoon, before dinnertime

WORST TIME TO GO
On a rainy day

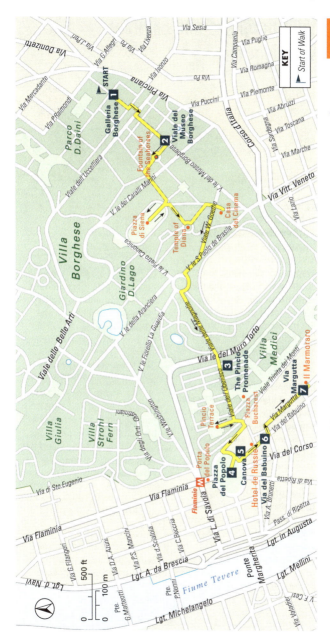

Two almost identical Baroque churches look out onto Piazza del Popolo.

Temple of Diana; and the Casa del Cinema, which screens films and hosts other film-related events.

3 Follow Via delle Magnolie and cross the little bridge over Viale del Muro Torto to reach the Pincio Promenade. The Pincio gardens have long been a beloved place for a walk and still give off an air of the Grand Tour, thanks to the marble busts of Italian Risorgimento heroes and artists that line the pathways. Note the vintage water clock designed in 1867, then continue west past Piazza Bucharest to the Pincio Terrace. There you'll be rewarded with breathtaking views of Piazza del Popolo. The setting is especially magical at sunset.

4 Descend the staircase on the right side of the Pincio Terrace, and in a few minutes, you'll reach Piazza del Popolo. Once the northern gateway to the city, the huge round plaza bustles with passersby for most of the day. In the center of the piazza, you can admire the Egyptian obelisk and the fountain with sphinxes spouting water from their mouths. It's also a good place to rest your feet if you need a break. If you stand with your back to the Medieval Porta del Popolo, you can gaze straight down Via del Corso and see all the way to the Vittoriano about a mile away.

5 You've earned an aperitivo, so take a seat at one of the tables at Canova overlooking the piazza. This Roman stalwart was a favored haunt of filmmaker Federico Fellini, who lived nearby on Via Margutta and supposedly had an office in the back of the *caffè*. Inside, in the hallway leading to the bathroom and a rear dining room, you can see his drawings and stills from his films. The food and drinks are just fine—nothing extraordinary—but the reason to patronize Canova is to soak up the atmosphere and do some people-watching, a quintessential Roman experience.

6 Once you've finished at Canova, start walking south on Via del Babuino, one of the three streets that branches off from Piazza del Popolo, forming a trident.

7 Stroll past Hotel de Russie and turn left onto Via Margutta. Though it's parallel to Via del Babuino, many people miss this charming cobblestone street. Known as the artists' street, it has long been a haven for artists and galleries. Picasso stayed here in the same building where some scenes of *Roman Holiday* starring Audrey Hepburn and Gregory Peck were filmed. Fellini lived at number 110, marked by a marble plaque dedicated to him and his wife Giulietta Masina. You can see where the plaque was made at Il Marmoraro, a sign shop at number 53B. There, Sandro Fiorentino still carves marble plaques by hand just like his father, who opened the shop in 1969, did.

The Pincio Terrace

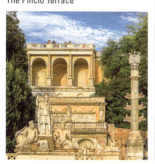

NEIGHBORHOOD SNAPSHOT

TOP EXPERIENCES

■ **Piazza del Popolo:** At the end of three of the *centro storico*'s most important streets—Via del Babuino, Via del Corso, and Via di Ripetta—the "People's Plaza" provides a front-row seat for some of Rome's best people-watching.

■ **Villa Borghese:** Drink in the fresh air in central Rome's largest park—stretches of green and plenty of leafy pathways encourage wandering, biking, or just chilling out.

■ **Galleria Borghese:** Appreciate the extravagant interior decor in one of Rome's most opulent and pleasant museums.

■ **Bernini's** *Ecstasy of St. Teresa* : Admire the worldly realism of Teresa's allegedly spiritual rapture. The star of the Cappella Cornaro at Santa Maria della Vittoria, Bernini's theatrical masterpiece is a cornerstone of the high Roman Baroque period.

■ **Capuchin Crypt:** Contemplate eternity in the creepy-yet-creative crypt under Santa Maria della Concezione, "decorated" with the skeletons of 4,000 friars, replete with fluted arches made of collarbones and arabesques of shoulder blades.

■ **Piazza del Quirinale:** Crowning the Quirinale—the loftiest of Rome's seven hills—is the Piazza del Quirinale, with spectacular views over the city. Its horizon is marked by "Il Cupolino," the dome of St. Peter's. Framing the vista are enormous ancient statues of Castor and Pollux, the Dioscuri (Horse-Tamers).

GETTING HERE

■ The Metro stop for Piazza del Popolo is Flaminio on Line A. The Villa Giulia, the Galleria Nazionale d'Arte Moderna e Contemporanea, and the Bioparco in Villa Borghese are accessible from Via Flaminia, and are about 1 km (½ mile) from Piazza del Popolo. Tram No. 19 stops at each. Bus No. 628 connects Piazza del Popolo to Piazza Venezia. Buses No. 61 and 160 go into Villa Borghese.

■ Located between Termini station and the Spanish Steps, Repubblica is about a 15-minute walk from either. Bus No. 40 will get you from Termini to the Quirinale in two stops; from the Vatican, take Bus No. 64. The very central Repubblica Metro stop is on the piazza of the same name.

The area north and east of the Trevi Fountain and Piazza di Spagna comprises a handful of neighborhoods that Romans consider very central but tourists sometimes miss. One of the city's most showstopping piazzas is here: the large round Piazza del Popolo, once the northern gateway to the city. Just uphill from it is the Pincio and Villa Borghese. To the east lie the Quirinal Hill and Piazza della Repubblica, which contain more than their fair share of Baroque masterpieces.

It may not feel like it amid the centro storico's warren of cobblestone streets, but Rome is a very green city. All around the immediate city center are vast public parks, the most central of which is the city's giant green lung: the Villa Borghese park, where residents love to escape to for some serious R&R. But don't think you can completely avoid sightseeing—three of Rome's most important museums are inside the park, and Piazza del Popolo, which has more than one art-crammed church, is close by.

Just northwest of Termini station, Repubblica and the Quirinale offer an extraordinary Roman blend of old and new. The stretch from Piazza della Repubblica to Piazza Barberini swarms with professionals going in and out of office buildings, as the Quirinale, home to the president of Italy, buzzes with political activity. It's more than just a workaday area, though, with intriguing attractions ranging from the bizarre Capuchin Crypt to great Bernini sculptures.

Sights

★ Galleria Borghese
ART MUSEUM | It's toss-up as to which is more magnificent: the museum or the art that lies within it. The luxury-loving Cardinal Scipione Borghese had the museum custom built in 1612 as a showcase for his collection of both antiquities and more

Principessa Pauline Borghese, Napoléon's sister, scandalized Europe by posing as a half-naked Venus for Canova; the statue is on view at the Galleria Borghese.

"modern" works, including those he commissioned from the masters Caravaggio and Bernini. Today, it's a monument to Roman interior decoration at its most extravagant.

One of the collection's most famous works is Canova's Neoclassical sculpture, *Pauline Borghese as Venus Victorious*. The next three rooms hold three key early Baroque sculptures: Bernini's *David*; *Apollo and Daphne*; and *The Rape of Persephone*. All were done when the artist was in his twenties and all illustrate his extraordinary skill. *Apollo and Daphne* shows the moment when, to aid her escape from the pursuing Apollo, Daphne is turned into a laurel tree. Leaves and twigs sprout from her fingertips as she stretches agonizingly away from Apollo. In *The Rape of Persephone*, Pluto has either just plucked Persephone (or Proserpina) from her flower-picking or is in the process of returning to Hades with his prize. Note the realistic way his grip causes dimples in Persephone's flesh. This is the stuff that makes the Baroque exciting—and moving. Other Berninis on view include a large, unfinished figure called *Verità*, or Truth.

Room 8 contains six paintings by Caravaggio, the hotheaded genius who died at age 37. All of his paintings, even the charming *Boy with a Basket of Fruit*, have an undercurrent of darkness. The disquieting *Sick Bacchus* is a self-portrait of the artist who, like the god, had a fondness for wine. *David and Goliath*, painted in the last year of Caravaggio's life—while he was on the run, murder charges hanging over his head—includes his self-portrait in the head of Goliath. Upstairs, the Pinacoteca (Picture Gallery) boasts paintings by Raphael (including his moving *Deposition*), Pinturicchio, Perugino, Bellini, and Rubens. Probably the gallery's most famous painting is Titian's allegorical *Sacred and Profane Love*, a mysterious image with two female figures, one nude, one clothed. ■**TIP→ Admission to the Galleria Borghese is by reservation only. Visitors are admitted in two-hour shifts 9–5. Prime-time slots sell out days in advance, so reserve directly (and early) through the museum's website.** ✉ *Piazzale Scipione Borghese, 5, off Via Pinciana, Villa Borghese* ☎ *06/32810 reservations, 06/8413979 info* ⊕ *www.galleriaborghese.beniculturali.it* 🖃 *€15, including €2 reservation fee; increased fee during temporary exhibitions* ⊗ *Closed Mon.* ⚐ *Reservations essential.*

★ Galleria Nazionale d'Arte Moderna e Contemporanea (*National Gallery of Modern Art*)

ART MUSEUM | This massive white Beaux-Arts building, built for the 1911 World Exposition in Rome, contains one of Italy's leading collections of 19th- and 20th-century works. It's primarily dedicated to the history of Italian modernism, examining the movement's development over the last two centuries, but crowd-pleasers Monet, Rodin, Van Gogh, and Warhol put in appearances, and there's also an outstanding Dadaist collection. You can mix coffee and culture at the mid-century-inspired Caffè delle Arti in a columned alcove. ✉ *Viale delle Belle Arti, 131, Villa Borghese* ☎ *06/32298221* ⊕ *www.lagallerianazionale.com* 🖃 *€10* ⊗ *Closed Mon.* Ⓜ *Flaminio.*

★ MACRO

ART MUSEUM | Formerly known as Rome's Modern and Contemporary Art Gallery, and before that as the Peroni beer factory, this redesigned industrial space has brought new life to the gallery and museum scene of a city hitherto hailed for its "then," not its "now." The collection here covers Italian contemporary artists from the 1960s through today. The goal is to bring current art to the public in innovative spaces and, not incidentally, to support and recognize Rome's contemporary art scene, which labors in the shadow of the city's artistic heritage. After a few days—or millennia—of dusty marble, it's a breath of fresh air. ■**TIP→ Check the website for occasional late-night openings and events.** ✉ *Via Nizza, 138, Repubblica* ☎ *06/696271* ⊕ *www.museomacro.it* 🖃 *Free* ⊗ *Closed Mon.* Ⓜ *Castro Pretorio.*

★ MAXXI—Museo Nazionale delle Arti del XXI Secolo (*National Museum of 21st-Century Arts*)

ART MUSEUM | Designed by the late Iraqi-British architect Zaha Hadid, this modern building plays with lots of natural light and has curving and angular lines, big open spaces, glass ceilings, and

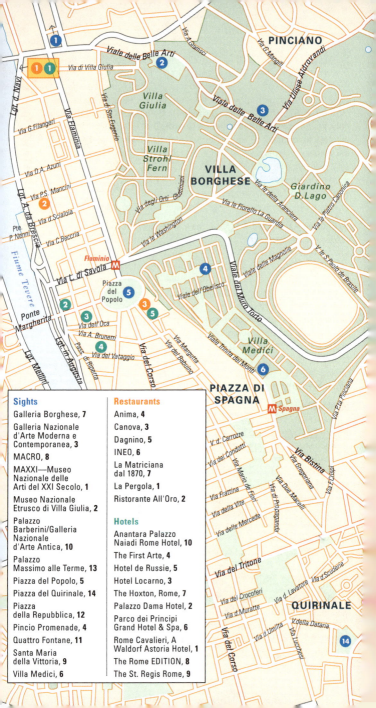

steel staircases that twist through the air—all meant to question the division between "within" and "without." The MAXXI hosts temporary exhibitions of art, architecture, film, and more. The permanent collection, displayed on a rotating basis, has more than 350 works from modern and contemporary artists, including Andy Warhol, Francesco Clemente, and Gerhard Richter. ✉ *Via Guido Reni, 4/A, Flaminio* ☎ *06/3201954* ⊕ *www.maxxi.art* 🎟 *€15* ⊘ *Closed Mon.* Ⓜ *Flaminio, then Tram No. 2 to Apollodoro.*

★ Museo Nazionale Etrusco di Villa Giulia (*National Etruscan Museum*)

ART MUSEUM | The world's most outstanding collection of Etruscan art and artifacts is housed in Villa Giulia, built around 1551 for Pope Julius III. Among the team called in to plan and construct the villa were Michelangelo and fellow Florentine Vasari. Most of the actual work, however, was done by Vignola and Ammannati. The villa's *nymphaeum*—or sunken sculpture garden—is a superb example of a refined late-Renaissance setting for princely pleasures.

No one knows precisely where the Etruscans originated, but many scholars maintain they came from Asia Minor, appearing in Italy about 2000 BC and creating a civilization that was a dazzling prelude to that of the ancient Romans. Among the most striking pieces are the terra-cotta statues, such as the *Apollo of Veii* and the serenely beautiful *Sarcophagus of the Spouses*. Dating from 530–500 BC, this couple (or Sposi) look at the viewer with almond eyes and archaic smiles, suggesting an openness and joie de vivre rare in Roman art. Other highlights include the cinematic frieze from a later temple (480 BC) in Pyrgi, resembling a sort of Etruscan Elgin marbles in terra-cotta; the displays of Etruscan jewelry; and the beautiful gardens. ✉ *Piazzale di Villa Giulia, 9, Villa Borghese* ☎ *06/3226571* ⊕ *www.museoetru.it* 🎟 *€12* ⊘ *Closed Mon.*

★ Palazzo Barberini/Galleria Nazionale d'Arte Antica

ART MUSEUM | One of Rome's most splendid 17th-century buildings is a Baroque landmark. The grand facade was designed by Carlo Maderno (aided by his nephew, Francesco Borromini), but when Maderno died, Borromini was passed over in favor of his great rival, Gian Lorenzo Bernini. The palazzo is now home to the Galleria Nazionale d'Arte Antica, with a collection that includes Raphael's *La Fornarina*, a luminous portrait of the artist's lover (a resident of Trastevere, she was reputedly a baker's daughter). Also noteworthy are Guido Reni's portrait of the doomed Beatrice Cenci (beheaded in Rome for patricide in 1599)—Hawthorne called it "the saddest picture ever painted" in his Rome-based novel, *The Marble Faun*—and Caravaggio's dramatic *Judith Beheading Holofernes*.

The showstopper here is the palace's Gran Salone, a vast ballroom with a ceiling painted in 1630 by the third (and too-often-neglected) master of the Roman Baroque, Pietro da Cortona. It depicts the *Glorification of Urban VIII's Reign* and has the spectacular conceit of glorifying Urban VIII as the agent of Divine Providence, escorted by a "bomber squadron" (to quote art historian Sir Michael Levey) of huge Barberini bees, the heraldic symbol of the family. ✉ *Via delle Quattro Fontane, 13, Quirinale* ☎ *06/4814591* ⊕ *www.barberinicorsini.org* 🎟 *€12, includes Galleria Corsini* ⊙ *Closed Mon.* Ⓜ *Barberini.*

★ Palazzo Massimo alle Terme

ART MUSEUM | The Museo Nazionale Romano, with items ranging from striking classical Roman paintings to marble bric-a-brac, has four locations: Palazzo Altemps, Crypta Balbi, the Museo delle Terme di Diocleziano, and this, the Palazzo Massimo alle Terme—a vast structure containing the great ancient treasures of the archaeological collection and also the coin collection. Highlights include the *Dying Niobid*, the famous bronze *Boxer at Rest*, and the *Discobolus Lancellotti*.

Among the museum's most intriguing attractions, however, are the ancient frescoes on view on the top floor. They're stunningly set up to "re-create" the look of the homes they once decorated, and their colors are remarkably preserved. You'll see stuccoes and wall paintings found in the area of the Villa Farnesina (in Trastevere), as well as those depicting a garden in bloom and an orchard alive with birds that once covered the walls of cool sunken rooms at Empress Livia's villa in Prima Porta, just outside the city. ✉ *Largo di Villa Peretti, 2, Repubblica* ☎ *06/39967700* ⊕ *www.museonazionaleromano.beniculturali.it* 🎟 *€10, or €14 for a combined ticket including access to Crypta Balbi, Museo delle Terme di Diocleziano, and Palazzo Altemps (valid for 1 wk)* ⊙ *Closed Mon.* Ⓜ *Repubblica, Termini.*

Piazza della Repubblica

PLAZA/SQUARE | Often the first view that spells "Rome" to weary travelers walking from Termini station, this round piazza was laid out in the late 1800s and follows the line of the caldarium of the vast ancient public baths, the Terme di Diocleziano. At its center, the exuberant Fontana delle Naiadi (Fountain of the Naiads) teems with voluptuous bronze ladies happily wrestling with marine monsters. The nudes weren't there when the pope unveiled the fountain in 1888—sparing him any embarrassment—but when the figures were added in 1901, they caused a scandal. It's said that the sculptor, Mario Rutelli, modeled them on the ample figures of two musical-comedy stars of the day. The colonnades now house the luxe hotel Anantara Palazzo Naiadi and various shops and caffès. ✉ *Repubblica* Ⓜ *Repubblica*.

★ Piazza del Popolo

PLAZA/SQUARE | FAMILY | With its obelisk and twin churches, this immense square marks what was, for centuries, Rome's northern entrance, where all roads from the north converged and where visitors, many of them pilgrims, got their first impression of the Eternal City. The desire to make this entrance to Rome something special was a pet project of popes and their architects for more than three centuries. Although it was once crowded with fashionable carriages, the piazza today is a pedestrian zone. At election time, it's the scene of huge political rallies, and on New Year's Eve, Rome stages a mammoth alfresco party here. ✉ *Piazza del Popolo* Ⓜ *Flaminio*.

Piazza del Quirinale

PLAZA/SQUARE | This strategic location atop the Quirinale has long been important. Indeed, it served as home of the Sabines in the 7th century BC—when they were deadly enemies of the Romans, who lived on the Campidoglio and Palatino (all of 1 km [½ mile] away). Today, it's the foreground for the presidential residence, Palazzo del Quirinale, and home to the Palazzo della Consulta, where Italy's Constitutional Court sits.

The open side of the piazza has a vista over the rooftops and domes of central Rome and St. Peter's. The Fontana di Montecavallo, or Fontana dei Dioscuri, has a statuary group of Dioscuri trying to tame two massive marble steeds that was found in the Baths of Constantine, which once occupied part of the Quirinale's summit. Unlike many ancient statues in Rome, this group survived the Dark Ages intact, becoming one of the city's great sights during the Middle Ages. The obelisk next to the figures is from the Mausoleo di Augusto (Tomb of Augustus) and was put here by Pope Pius VI in the late 18th century. ✉ *Piazza del Quirinale, Quirinale* Ⓜ *Barberini*.

★ Pincio Promenade

VIEWPOINT | FAMILY | Redolent of the era of Henry James and Edith Wharton, the Pincian gardens have long been a classic setting for a walk. Grand Tourists—and even a pope or two—came here to see and be seen among the beau monde of Rome. Today, the Pincian terrace remains a favorite spot for locals taking a springtime Sunday stroll. The rather formal, early-19th-century style contrasts with the far more elaborate terraced gardens of Lucullus, the Roman gourmand who held legendary banquets here. Today, off-white marble busts of Italian Risorgimento heroes and artists line the pathways. Along with similar busts on the Gianicolo (Janiculum Hill), their noses have been targets of vandalism.

A stretch of ancient walls separates the Pincio from the southwest corner of Villa Borghese. From the balustraded terrace, you can look down at Piazza del Popolo and beyond, surveying much of Rome. Southeast of the Pincian terrace is the Casina Valadier (⊕ *www.casinavaladier.it*), a magnificently decorated Neoclassical building that contains an event space with glorious views. ✉ *Piazzale Napoleone I and Viale dell'Obelisco, Villa Borghese* Ⓜ *Flaminio*.

★ Santa Maria della Vittoria

CHURCH | Designed by Carlo Maderno, this church is best known for Bernini's sumptuous Baroque decoration of the Cappella Cornaro (Cornaro Chapel, the last on the left as you face the altar), which houses his interpretation of divine love in the *Ecstasy of St. Teresa*. Bernini's masterly fusion of sculpture, light, architecture, painting, and relief is a multimedia extravaganza, with the chapel modeled as a theater, and one of the key examples of the Roman High Baroque. The members of the Cornaro family meditate on the communal vision of the great moment of divine love before them: the swooning saint's robes appear to be on fire, quivering with life, and the white marble group seems suspended in the heavens as golden rays illuminate the scene. An angel assists as Teresa abandons herself to the joys of heavenly love. To modern eyes, Bernini's representation of the saint's experience may seem more earthly than mystical. As the visiting French dignitary Charles de Brosses put it in the 18th century, "If this is divine love, I know all about it." ✉ *Via XX Settembre, 17, Largo Santa Susanna, Repubblica* ☎ *06/42740571* Ⓜ *Repubblica*.

Quattro Fontane (*Four Fountains*)

VIEWPOINT | This intersection takes its name from its four Baroque fountains, which represent the Tiber (on the San Carlo corner), the Arno, Juno, and Diana. Despite the nearby traffic and the tightness of the sidewalk, it's worth taking in the views in all four directions from this point: to the southwest, as far as the obelisk in Piazza del Quirinale; to the northeast, along Via XX Settembre to the Porta Pia; to the northwest, across Piazza Barberini to the obelisk of Trinità dei Monti; and to the southeast, as far as the obelisk and apse of Santa Maria Maggiore. The prospect is a highlight of Pope Sixtus V's campaign of urban beautification and an example of Baroque influence on city planning. ✉ *Intersection of Via Quattro Fontane, Via XX Settembre, and Via del Quirinale, Quirinale* Ⓜ *Barberini*.

Villa Medici (*The French Academy of Rome*)
HISTORIC HOME | Originally belonging to Cardinal Ferdinando I de' Medici, who also laid out the immaculate Renaissance garden to set off his sculpture collection, this villa was purchased by Napoléon to create the French Academy of Rome, opened in 1803, where artists could study Italian art and put it toward the (French) national good. You can visit during special exhibitions or take a guided tour to see the gardens and the incredibly picturesque garden facade, which is studded with Mannerist and Rococo sculpted reliefs and overlooks a loggia with a beautiful fountain devoted to Mercury. Some of the historic rooms have been restyled by Fendi and Paris-based designer India Mahdavi. ✉ *Viale della Trinità dei Monti, 1, Villa Borghese* ☎ *06/6761200* ⊕ *www.villamedici.it* 🎫 *€10, exhibits; €14, includes guided tour of the gardens and historic rooms and exhibit* ⊘ *Closed Tues.* Ⓜ *Spagna.*

🍴 Restaurants

★ Anima
$$$$ | **MODERN ITALIAN** | Paola Colucci, the self-taught chef of beloved local restaurant Pianostrada, has brought her refined approach to comfort food to this buzzy restaurant in the Rome EDITION hotel. Be sure to request a table in the garden and don't skip the focaccia—baked fresh and topped with delicious things like gorgonzola, pears, cinnamon, arugula, and mint—before moving on to the fresh pasta. **Known for:** pillowy focaccia topped with gourmet ingredients; superlative pastas; beautifully presented dishes. 💲 *Average main: €38* ✉ *The Rome EDITION, Salita di S. Nicola da Tolentino, 14, Quirinale* ☎ *06/45249009* ⊕ *www.animaristoranteroma.it* Ⓜ *Barberini.*

Canova
$$ | **ITALIAN | FAMILY** | Esteemed director Federico Fellini, who lived around the corner on Via Margutta, used to come here all the time and even had an office in the back. His drawings and black-and-white stills from his films remain on display in the hallway that leads to the interior dining room, but the best place to sit for people-watching with a coffee, light lunch, or aperitivo is on the terrace out front. **Known for:** great people-watching; sandwiches and other light fare; Fellini's old hangout. 💲 *Average main: €15* ✉ *Piazza del Popolo, 16, Piazza del Popolo* ☎ *06/3612231* ⊕ *www.canovapiazzadelpopolo.it* Ⓜ *Flaminio.*

Dagnino
$ | **BAKERY** | Hidden inside a covered arcade, this Sicilian pasticceria, which opened in 1955, has pastry cases filled with cannoli, cassata, cakes, and marzipan as well as savory items like

sandwiches and arancini. Go for breakfast, and try the cornetto filled with ricotta and chocolate chips—this might be the only place in Rome where you can find it. **Known for:** Sicilian desserts; mid-century-modern design; cornetti filled with ricotta and chocolate chips. ⑤ *Average main: €3* ✉ *Via Vittorio Emanuele Orlando, 75, Repubblica* ☎ *06/4818660* ⊕ *www.dagnino.com* Ⓜ *Repubblica*.

★ INEO

$$$$ | **MODERN ITALIAN** | It's only a matter of time before this elegant restaurant inside the Anantara Palazzo Naiadi Hotel gets a Michelin star. With a chic, modern design, creative tasting menus by chef Heros De Agostinis, and special touches like a roving cart with a variety of delicious bread made in-house, this is a true five-star experience. **Known for:** gourmet tasting menus; globally influenced dishes; romantic ambience. ⑤ *Average main: €48* ✉ *Anantara Palazzo Naiadi, Piazza della Repubblica, 46, Repubblica* ☎ *06/489381* ⊕ *www.ineorestaurant.com* ⊗ *Closed Sun. and Mon.* Ⓜ *Repubblica*.

★ La Matriciana dal 1870

$$ | **ROMAN** | This old-school Roman restaurant traces its roots back to 1870, when a woman from the town of Amatrice in northern Lazio arrived in Rome and started to cook her town's renowned bucatini *all'amatriciana* near Termini Station. Whether the story is true or a legend, this is indeed a great place to try the famous pasta and other Roman specialties in an elegant space with white tablecloths, plates emblazoned with the restaurant's name, and courteous and formally attired waiters. **Known for:** bucatini all'amatriciana; elegant, old-school atmosphere; local favorite restaurant. ⑤ *Average main: €20* ✉ *Via del Viminale, 44, Repubblica* ☎ *06/4881775* ⊕ *www.lamatriciana.it* ⊗ *Closed Sat.* Ⓜ *Repubblica*.

★ La Pergola

$$$$ | **MODERN ITALIAN** | Dinner here is a truly spectacular and romantic event, with incomparable views across the city matched by a stellar dining experience that includes top-notch service as well as sublimely inventive fare. The difficulty comes in choosing from among Michelin-starred chef Heinz Beck's *alta cucina* (high cuisine) specialties. **Known for:** fagotelli La Pergola stuffed with pecorino, eggs, and cream with guanciale and zucchini; award-winning wine list; weekend reservations that book up three months in advance. ⑤ *Average main: €75* ✉ *Rome Cavalieri, A Waldorf Astoria Resort, Via Alberto Cadlolo, 101, Monte Mario* ☎ *06/35092152* ⊕ *www.romecavalieri.com* ⊗ *Closed Sun. and Mon., 3 wks in Jan., and 3 wks in Aug. No lunch* 🎩 *Jacket required*.

⭐ Ristorante All'Oro

$$$$ | MODERN ITALIAN | At this sleek Michelin-starred restaurant inside the Hall Tailor Suite hotel, chef/owner Riccardo Di Giacinto and his wife Ramona make fine dining a fun and entertaining experience. Di Giacinto worked with Ferran Adrià in Spain and uses some of his techniques without veering too far into the territory of molecular gastronomy. **Known for:** playful riffs on Roman dishes; top-notch service; sleek, modern design. ⑤ *Average main: €38* ✉ *Via Giuseppe Pisanelli, 25, Flaminio* ☎ *06/97996907* ⊕ *www.ristorantealloro.it* ⊘ *No lunch weekdays* Ⓜ *Flaminio.*

Hotels

Anantara Palazzo Naiadi Rome Hotel

$$$$ | HOTEL | You'll experience exquisite service and pampering at this Neoclassical landmark on the Piazza della Repubblica built on the foundations of the Baths of Diocletian—it's now run by Anantara, a luxury hotel brand with roots in Thailand. **Pros:** top-notch concierge and staff; multiple romantic dining options; spa with both Asian and European-style treatments. **Cons:** food and beverages are expensive; beyond the immediate vicinity of many sights; rooms are a different style than public spaces. ⑤ *Rooms from: €750* ✉ *Piazza della Repubblica, 47, Repubblica* ☎ *06/489381* ⊕ *www.anantara.com/en/palazzo-naiadi-rome* ⇌ *232 rooms* ⓄI *No Meals* Ⓜ *Repubblica, Termini.*

The First Arte

$$$$ | HOTEL | Set in a 19th-century Neoclassical palace, this cozy boutique hotel was remodeled to feature high-tech, elegant guest rooms while keeping the core structure, including unique windows and tall ceilings, intact. **Pros:** fitness room with Technogym equipment; staff that is eager to please; more than 200 works of art on display from Galleria Mucciaccia. **Cons:** some rooms can be dark; rooftop bar can get quite crowded; no spa. ⑤ *Rooms from: €500* ✉ *Via del Vantaggio, 14, Piazza del Popolo* ☎ *06/45617070* ⊕ *www.pavilionshotels.com/rome/thefirstarte* ⇌ *29 rooms* ⓄI *Free Breakfast* Ⓜ *Flaminio.*

⭐ Hotel de Russie

$$$$ | HOTEL | Occupying a 19th-century hotel that once hosted royalty, Picasso, and Cocteau, the Hotel de Russie is now the first choice in Rome for government bigwigs and Hollywood high rollers seeking ultimate luxury in a secluded retreat. **Pros:** big potential for celebrity sightings; well-equipped gym and world-class spa; excellent Stravinskij cocktail bar has outdoor tables on the Piazzetta Valadier. **Cons:** faster Internet comes at a fee; breakfast not included; very expensive. ⑤ *Rooms from: €1,700* ✉ *Via del*

Did You Know?

To increase the visual impact of the Ecstasy of St. Teresa, Bernini hid a window of yellow glass above the pediment to add iridescence to the gilded rays of "divine light."

Babuino, 9, Piazza del Popolo ☎ 06/328881 ⊕ www.roccofortehotels.com ⇌ 120 rooms ⫽❂⫽ No Meals Ⓜ Flaminio.

Hotel Locarno
$$$$ | **HOTEL** | Established in 1925, this hotel feels like an authentic time capsule of a more glamorous era. **Pros:** spacious rooms; complimentary bicycles; gym. **Cons:** some rooms are dark; cleaning fee of €40 per night for pets; food and drinks are expensive. ⑤ *Rooms from: €390* ✉ *Via della Penna, 22, Piazza del Popolo* ☎ *06/3610841* ⊕ *www.hotellocarno.com* ⇌ *49 rooms* ⫽❂⫽ *Free Breakfast* Ⓜ *Flaminio*.

The Hoxton, Rome
$$ | **HOTEL** | British brand The Hoxton's first foray into Italy is a design lover's dream filled with 1970s-inspired bespoke furniture, art tomes, and plants that transform the large lobby into intimate seating nooks perfect for socializing and coworking. **Pros:** stylish design; friendly staff; great food and drinks. **Cons:** far from main sights, with the closest Metro stop a mile away; rooms have little storage space for clothes; no gym or spa. ⑤ *Rooms from: €189* ✉ *Largo Benedetto Marcello, 220, Parioli* ☎ *06/94502700* ⊕ *www.thehoxton.com/rome* ⇌ *192 rooms* ⫽❂⫽ *No Meals*.

Palazzo Dama Hotel
$$$$ | **HOTEL** | This former Roman villa was once home to the Malaspina family, who hosted high society gatherings throughout the 18th century. **Pros:** drinks and bites available all-day in garden or main hall; Acqua di Parma toiletries; pool is open year-round. **Cons:** standard rooms are small with little storage space; room service is slow and portions are tiny; rooms can be noisy. ⑤ *Rooms from: €430* ✉ *Lungotevere Arnaldo da Brescia, 2, Flaminio* ☎ *06/89565272* ⊕ *www.palazzodama.com* ⇌ *29 rooms* ⫽❂⫽ *Free Breakfast* Ⓜ *Flaminio*.

Parco dei Principi Grand Hotel & Spa
$$$$ | **HOTEL** | The 1960s-era facade of this large, seven-story hotel designed by Gio Ponti contrasts with the turn-of-the-20th-century Italian court decor and the extensive botanical garden outside, resulting in a combination of traditional elegance and contemporary pleasure. **Pros:** quiet location on Villa Borghese; fitness room with wide variety of equipment; biosauna and sensory showers at spa. **Cons:** extra charge to use the pool; bathrooms could use an update; a bit of a hike to caffès and restaurants. ⑤ *Rooms from: €450* ✉ *Via Gerolamo Frescobaldi, 5, Villa Borghese* ☎ *06/854421* ⊕ *www.parcodeiprincipi.com* ⇌ *177 rooms* ⫽❂⫽ *Free Breakfast*.

Rome Cavalieri, A Waldorf Astoria Hotel

$$$$ | **RESORT** | **FAMILY** | Set in a quiet residential neighborhood amid 15 acres of lush Mediterranean parkland, the Rome Cavalieri is a true hilltop oasis with magnificent views as well as three outdoor pools, one indoor pool, and a palatial spa. **Pros:** famed art collection, including a Tiepolo triptych from 1725; complimentary shuttle to city center; impressive on-site restaurant. **Cons:** you definitely pay for the luxury of staying here—everything is expensive; outside the city center; not all rooms have great views. *Rooms from: €420 ⊠ Via Alberto Cadlolo, 101, Monte Mario ☎ 06/3509 ⊕ www.romecavalieri.com ⇌ 370 rooms ⎮◎⎮ No Meals.*

★ The Rome EDITION

$$$$ | **HOTEL** | Set in a rationalist 1940s building that once housed the offices of the Banca Nazionale del Lavoro, this trendy lifestyle hotel by Ian Schrager and Marriott is one of the city's buzziest new places to stay. **Pros:** great location on a quiet street near Piazza Barberini; excellent dining and drinks; stylish interiors by renowned designer Patricia Urquiola. **Cons:** expensive; some rooms are quite small; service can be hit or miss. *Rooms from: €696 ⊠ Salita di S. Nicola da Tolentino, 14, Quirinale ☎ 06/45249000 ⊕ www.editionhotels.com ⇌ 91 rooms ⎮◎⎮ No Meals* Ⓜ *Barberini.*

The St. Regis Rome

$$$$ | **HOTEL** | Originally opened by César Ritz in 1894, this grande dame has a Belle Epoque lobby filled with classic and contemporary art, a ballroom with painstakingly restored ceiling frescoes, and an intimate library where you can sip a cup of tea or something stronger. **Pros:** houses the Roman location of international art gallery Galleria Continua; every room comes with 24/7 butler service; the library lounge serves a lovely afternoon tea. **Cons:** food and drinks are pricey; breakfast is not included; restaurant feels more like a lounge than a proper restaurant. *Rooms from: €800 ⊠ Via Vittorio E. Orlando, 3, Repubblica ☎ 06/47091 ⊕ www.marriott.com ⇌ 161 rooms ⎮◎⎮ No Meals* Ⓜ *Repubblica.*

Nightlife

Metropolita

COCKTAIL BARS | Conveniently close to MAXXI and the Auditorium Parco della Musica, this hip lounge serves classic and creative cocktails as well as light bites in a two-story space with tables on the mezzanine and low sofas on the ground floor. The tapas-style menu is international, with offerings like guacamole and hummus in addition to the popular *maritozzo salato*, a savory version of the

Roman bun filled with tuna instead of cream, and a few heartier options, including a burger. Food is served until 1 am every night, and brunch is available on weekends. ✉ *Piazza Gentile da Fabriano, 2, Flaminio* ☎ *06/84381895* ⊕ *www.metropolita.it.*

★ Stravinskij Bar at the Hotel de Russie

COCKTAIL BARS | The Stravinskij Bar, in the Hotel de Russie, is the best place to sample la dolce vita. Celebrities, blue bloods, and VIPs hang out in the gorgeous Piazzetta Valadier where mixed drinks and cocktails are well above par. There are also healthy smoothies and bites if you need to refuel. ✉ *Hotel de Russie, Via del Babuino, 9, Piazza del Popolo* ☎ *06/3288874* ⊕ *www.roccofortehotels.com* Ⓜ *Flaminio.*

Shopping

Esedra 58

CLOTHING | For gentlemen looking to bring home some Italian style, this family-run boutique under the arcades on Piazza della Repubblica is a must. You won't find designer names like Armani but rather small Italian producers like Gran Sasso, which makes high-quality knits, and Camplin, which makes the original Royal Navy peacoat. The in-house tailor is available to make quick adjustments. ✉ *Piazza della Repubblica, 58, Repubblica* ☎ *06/4814701* ⊕ *www.esedra58.it* Ⓜ *Repubblica.*

★ Il Marmoraro

SPECIALTY STORE | This tiny shop is a holdout of Via Margutta's days as a street full of artists and artisans. Sandro Fiorentino's father opened the shop in 1969 (he carved plaques like the one that marks Federico Fellini's house up the street), and Sandro still engraves the marble by hand. The shop is packed full of plaques, many with clever phrases, which make a great souvenir. Sandro will also engrave a message of your choice upon request. ✉ *Via Margutta, 53B, Piazza del Popolo* ☎ *335/6593612* Ⓜ *Spagna.*

Laura Urbinati

CLOTHING | Originally from Rome but now based in Milan, Laura Urbinati is a fashion designer whose swimwear has appeared on the pages of *Vogue, Elle, W,* and other magazines. At her namesake shop on a street just off Piazza del Popolo, you'll find colorful silk tops, pants, dresses, and skirts with bold prints and patterns in addition to the swimwear she's famous for. ✉ *Via dell'Oca, 48, Piazza del Popolo* ☎ *06/3214345* ⊕ *www.lauraurbinati.com* Ⓜ *Flaminio.*

Chapter 8

TRASTEVERE, TESTACCIO, AND ENVIRONS

Updated by
Laura Itzkowitz

⦿ Sights　🍴 Restaurants　🛏 Hotels　🛍 Shopping　🍸 Nightlife
★★☆☆☆　★★★★☆　★★☆☆☆　★★★★☆　★★★★☆

Trastevere and Testaccio Walking Tour

Though quickly gentrifying, Trastevere and Testaccio cling to their working-class roots. Both are known for restaurants and nightlife, but a daytime visit will reward you with fewer crowds and the chance to see sights only open in the mornings.

1 Begin the tour at Villa Farnesina located in Trastevere, one of Rome's most picturesque neighborhoods with winding cobblestone streets. The villa was built in the 16th century for the wealthy banker Agostino Chigi, who commissioned the greatest artists of the era—including Raphael—to paint frescoes, the most spectacular of which can be seen on the ceilings of the Loggia of Cupid and Psyche. It is only open in the mornings (last entry at 1:15 pm) from Monday to Saturday and is usually nearly empty, which makes it a great antidote to Rome's more crowded museums. You can see the whole villa in about 20 or 30 minutes.

2 Afterward, walk south on Via della Lungara. Just beyond the arch is supposedly where Raphael's lover—the daughter of a baker—lived.

3 Veer left onto Via di Santa Dorotea and you'll emerge onto Piazza Trilussa, the bustling square that serves as a gateway to the neighborhood. In

Walking Tour 101

HIGHLIGHTS
Villa Farnesina, Basilica di Santa Maria in Trastevere, Supplì, Testaccio Market

WHERE TO START
Villa Farnesina

LENGTH
1–2 hours, depending on your pace and how often you stop

WHERE TO END
Piramide di Caio Cestio

BEST TIME TO GO
In the late morning or early afternoon, around lunchtime; if you don't mind skipping Villa Farnesina and are content with the crowds, in the evening, when Trastevere's nightlife comes alive

WORST TIME TO GO
On a rainy day

169

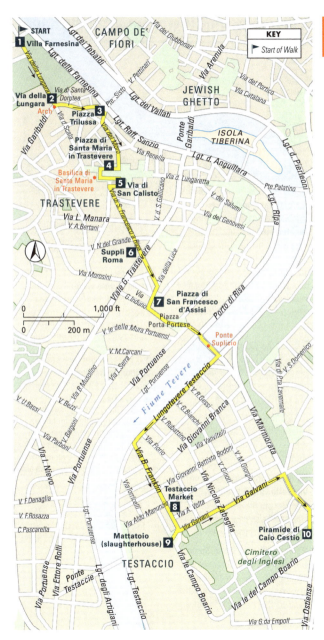

Piazza di Santa Maria in Trastevere is a peaceful stop to people-watch.

the evenings, street performers capture the attention of passersby and young people hang out on the steps drinking beer.

4 Cross the piazza and walk on Via del Moro for a few blocks, then turn right onto Via della Lungaretta, which leads to Piazza di Santa Maria in Trastevere. This lovely square surrounded by sidewalk *caffès* is great for people-watching, especially if you join the people sitting on the steps of the fountain. You can't miss the Basilica di Santa Maria in Trastevere, with its glittering mosaics. Inside, it contains yet more mosaics, columns from the Baths of Caracalla, and a gilded ceiling by Domenichino.

5 After you've seen the church, turn right onto Via di San Calisto, where you'll likely spot some street art. Follow the street's curves and continue onto Via di San Francesco a Ripa.

6 If you're ready for a snack, pop into Supplì Roma, a hole-in-the-wall spot known for some of the city's best street food. The namesake fried rice balls are the thing to order, but there are also other treats like fried cod or zucchini blossoms.

7 Take your snack to go and eat them on Piazza di San Francesco d'Assisi. Then cross the piazza and continue on toward Piazza di Porta Portese, which hosts a large open-air flea market on Sunday mornings.

8 **Cross the Ponte Suplicio and turn right onto Lungotevere Testaccio, walk a few blocks, then turn left onto Via Beniamino Franklin and follow it until you reach Testaccio Market.** This bustling covered market contains stalls where vendors sell fresh fruit, vegetables, meat, cheese, and fish, as well as places where you can get pizza or sandwiches. For a real taste of the neighborhood, stop by Mordi e Vai, where local specialties like tripe, tongue, or meatballs are stuffed into sandwich rolls. The market is open every day except Sunday until 2:30 pm.

9 **After lunch, continue your exploration of Testaccio, which was once home to Rome's slaughterhouse and is now a hip neighborhood full of street art, restaurants, and bars.** Note the *mattatoio* (slaughterhouse), which is being transformed into a cultural hub with a contemporary art gallery, caffè, and bookshop.

10 **Turn left onto Via Galvani and walk a few blocks. Then turn right onto Via Marmorata and you'll soon find yourself staring at the Piramide di Caio Cestio.** This massive pyramid was built in 12 BC for the wealthy praetor Gaius Cestius and was later incorporated into the Aurelian Walls built to protect the city—which is why it survived, while many other ancient pyramids were destroyed. It's very rarely open to the public, but it makes for a great photo opp and stands conveniently across from the Piramide metro stop.

Villa Farnesina

NEIGHBORHOOD SNAPSHOT

TOP REASONS TO GO

- **Santa Maria in Trastevere:** Tear yourself away from the ever-changing piazza scene outside to take in the gilded glory of one of the city's oldest and most beautiful churches, fabled for its medieval mosaics.

- **Isola Tiberina:** Cross the river on the Ponte Fabricio—the city's oldest bridge—for a stroll on the paved shores of the adorable Tiber Island (and don't forget to detour for the lemon ices at La Grattachecca kiosk on the Lungotevere).

- **Nightlife:** Trastevere is one of Rome's hottest nighttime-scene arenas, where people often spill out into the streets from the many lively bars.

- **Gran Priorato di Roma dell'Ordine di Malta:** Head to the compound of the Knights of Malta in Piazza Cavalieri di Malta to peek through the keyhole of a door and see a perfectly framed view of one of Rome's most famous landmarks.

- **Roseto Comunale:** Overlooking the Circo Massimo, this seasonal rose garden offers a fitting and fragrant vestibule to Rome's most poetic hill.

- **Baths of Caracalla:** South of the lovely Villa Celimontana Park are the imposing ruins of the Terme di Caracalla, once the second-largest bathing complex of the Roman world.

GETTING HERE

- From the Vatican or Spanish Steps, expect a 30- to 40-minute walk to reach Trastevere. From Termini Station, take Bus No. 40 Express or No. 64 to Largo di Torre Argentina, where you can switch to Tram No. 8 to get to Trastevere. The H bus will also take you directly from Termini Station to Trastevere and then Monteverde.

- From either the Roman Forum or the Campidoglio, it's a spectacular 20-minute walk through ancient ruins like the Circo Massimo to reach Aventino (the Aventine Hill). The Circo Massimo Metro stop puts you at the foot of the hill. If you're coming from the Colosseum or Trastevere, take Tram No. 3; from the Spanish Steps, take Bus No. 160.

- For Testaccio, use the Piramide (Ostiense) Metro stop.

Just beyond the busy *centro storico* lie the neighborhoods of Trastevere, Monteverde, Aventino, and Testaccio, each one unique and worth exploring. Trastevere and Testaccio—separated by the Tiber—were once working-class neighborhoods and today are among the city's buzziest areas for restaurants and nightlife. Aventino and Monteverde, each of which was built high on a hill, are leafy, residential neighborhoods where you can get an authentic feel for how Romans live today.

Trastevere ("beyond the Tiber") can feel a world apart from the rest of Rome, and, despite galloping gentrification, the bohemian neighborhood remains about the most tightly knit community in the city. Although grand art awaits at Santa Maria in Trastevere and the Villa Farnesina, the neighborhood's greatest attraction is simply its atmosphere.

Perfectly picturesque piazzas, tiny winding medieval alleyways, and time-burnished Romanesque houses cast a frozen-in-history spell. Traditional shops line crooked streets that are peaceful during the day and alive with throngs of people at night. From here, a steep hike up stairs and along the road to the Gianicolo, Rome's second-highest hill, earns you a panoramic view of the city.

Farther uphill, along the No. 8 Tram line, Monteverde—with its sprawling parks and typical residential lanes—is a quiet contrast to the bustle of trendy Trastevere. This area has also become a destination for its growing culinary scene.

Although Romans consider Trastevere, Monteverde, Aventino, and Testaccio to be central neighborhoods, they're just far enough off the beaten path to be little known to visitors—and to have retained their unique character. If you have extra time, a visit to these areas allows a glimpse into a more lived-in Eternal City— from the well-heeled, garden-filled residential quarter of Aventino to the traditional-yet-trendy riverside neighborhood of Testaccio.

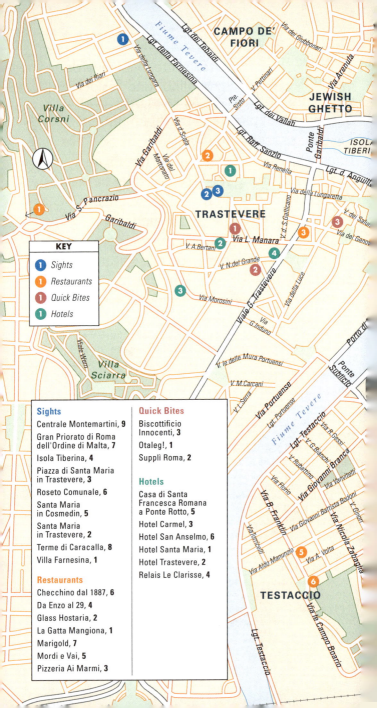

Sights

★ Centrale Montemartini

ART MUSEUM | A decommissioned early-20th-century power plant is now this intriguing exhibition space for the overflow of ancient art from the Musei Capitolini collection. Getting here is half the fun. A 15-minute walk from the heart of Testaccio will lead you past walls covered in street art to the urban district of Ostiense. Head southwest and saunter under the train tracks passing buildings adorned with four-story-high murals until you reach the often-uncrowded Centrale Montemartini, where Roman sculptures and mosaics are set amid industrial machinery and pipes.

Unusually, the collection is organized by the area in which the ancient pieces were found. Highlights include the former boiler room filled with ancient marble statues that once decorated Rome's private villas, such as the beautiful *Esquiline Venus*, as well as a large mosaic of a hunting scene. ■**TIP→ A purchase of the Capitolini Card will allow entry into Musei Capitolini and Centrale Montemartini.** ✉ *Via Ostiense, 106, Testaccio* ☎ *06/0608* ⊕ *www.centralemontemartini.org* 💶 *€11.50; admission included with the purchase of the Capitolini Card (€14.50)* ⊘ *Closed Mon.* Ⓜ *Garbatella*.

★ Gran Priorato di Roma dell'Ordine di Malta

RELIGIOUS BUILDING | **FAMILY** | Although the line to peek through the keyhole of a nondescript green door in the Gran Priorato, the walled compound of the Knights of Malta, sometimes snakes around Piazza dei Cavalieri di Malta, the enchanting view is worth the wait. Far across the city, you'll see the dome of St. Peter's Basilica flawlessly framed by the keyhole and tidily trimmed hedges that lie just beyond the locked door. The priory and the square are the work of Giovanni Battista Piranesi, an 18th-century engraver who is more famous for etching Roman views than for orchestrating them, but he fancied himself a bit of an architect and did not disappoint.

Founded in the Holy Land during the Crusades, the Knights of Malta is the world's oldest and most exclusive order of chivalry. The knights amassed huge tracts of land in the Middle East and were based on the Mediterranean island of Malta from 1530 until 1798, when Napoléon expelled them. In 1834, they established themselves in Rome, where ministering to the sick became their raison d'être. ■**TIP→ Private, guided tours of the Gran Priorato are usually offered on Friday morning, but you must prebook by email.** ✉ *Via Santa Sabina and Via Porta Lavernale, Aventino* ⊕ *www.ordinedimaltaitalia.org/gran-priorato-di-roma* ✉ *visitorscentre@*

orderofmalta.int 🖃 *From €5 per person (10 people minimum), plus the cost of the required guide, €80 in Italian, €100 in any other language. If a group has already formed, then anyone may join for the regular entry fee* ⊙ *Villa closed July, Aug., and Dec.* ⚐ *Reservations required* Ⓜ *Circo Massimo; Tram No. 3.*

Isola Tiberina (*Tiber Island*)

ISLAND | FAMILY | It's easy to overlook this tiny island in the Tiber, but you shouldn't. In terms of history and sheer loveliness, charming Isola Tiberina—shaped like a boat about to set sail—gets high marks. Cross onto the island via Ponte Fabricio, Rome's oldest remaining bridge, constructed in 62 BC. On the north side of the island crumbles the romantic ruin of the Ponte Rotto (Broken Bridge), which dates from 179 BC. Descend the steps to the lovely river embankment to see a Roman relief of the intertwined-snakes symbol of Aesculapius, the great god of healing.

In imperial times, Romans sheathed the entire island with marble to make it look like Aesculapius's ship, replete with a towering obelisk as a mast. Amazingly, a fragment of the ancient sculpted ship's prow still exists. You can marvel at it on the downstream end of the embankment. Today, medicine still reigns here. The island is home to the hospital of Fatebenefratelli (literally, "Do good, brothers"). Nearby is San Bartolomeo, built at the end of the 10th century by the Holy Roman Emperor Otto III and restored in the 18th century.

During summer, the island hosts an outdoor cinema while its rim is dotted with white tented bars and pop-up eateries. 🖃 *Trastevere* ✣ *Isola Tiberina can be accessed by Ponte Fabricio or Ponte Cestio.*

Piazza di Santa Maria in Trastevere

PLAZA/SQUARE | FAMILY | At the very heart of the Trastevere *rione* (district) lies this beautiful piazza, with its elegant raised fountain and sidewalk caffès. The centerpiece is the 12th-century church of Santa Maria in Trastevere, first consecrated in the 4th century. Across countless generations, this piazza has seen the comings and goings of residents and travelers, as well as intellectuals and artists, who today often lounge on the steps of the fountain or eat lunch at an outdoor table at Sabatini's. At night, the piazza is the center of Trastevere's action, with street festivals, musicians, and the occasional mime vying for attention from the many people taking the evening air. 🖃 *Piazza di Santa Maria in Trastevere, Trastevere.*

Roseto Comunale

GARDEN | As suggested by the paths shaped like a menorah, this was once a Jewish cemetery. All but one tombstone was moved, and the space is now a municipal garden that is open during the few weeks in the warmer months when the roses are in bloom. The garden is laid out to reflect the history of roses from antiquity to the present day and features more than 1,000 varieties. Its location also offers sweeping views across the old chariot track of the Circus Maximus. ✉ *Viale di Valle Murcia, Rome* ✪ *Closed July–late Apr.* Ⓜ *Circo Massimo. Bus Nos. 60, 81, 118, 160, 271, 628, and 715; Tram No. 3.*

★ Santa Maria in Cosmedin

CHURCH | FAMILY | One of Rome's oldest churches—built in the 6th century and restored in the late 19th century—is on the Piazza della Bocca della Verità, originally the location of the Forum Boarium, ancient Rome's cattle market and later the site of public executions. Although the church has a haunting interior and contains the flower-crowned skull of St. Valentine, who is celebrated every February 14th, it plays second fiddle to the renowned artifact installed out in its portico.

The Bocca della Verità (Mouth of Truth) is in reality nothing more than an ancient drain cover, unearthed during the Middle Ages. Legend has it, however, that the teeth will clamp down on a liar's hand if they dare to tell a fib while holding their fingers up to the fearsome mouth. Hordes of tourists line up to take the test every day (kids especially get a kick out of it). ✉ *Piazza della Bocca della Verità, 18, Aventino* ☎ *06/6787759* ⊕ *www.cosmedin.org* Ⓜ *Circo Massimo.*

★ Santa Maria in Trastevere

CHURCH | Built during the 4th century and rebuilt in the 12th century, this is one of Rome's oldest and grandest churches. It is also the earliest foundation of any Roman church to be dedicated to the Virgin Mary. The 18th-century portico draws attention to the facade's 800-year-old mosaics, which represent the parable of the Wise and Foolish Virgins. They enhance the whole piazza, especially at night, when the church front and bell tower are illuminated.

With a nave framed by a processional of two rows of gigantic columns (22 in total) taken from the ancient Baths of Caracalla, and an apse studded with gilded mosaics, the interior conjures the splendor of ancient Rome. Overhead is Domenichino's gilded ceiling (1617). The church's most important mosaics, Pietro Cavallini's six panels of the *Life of the Virgin*, cover the semicircular apse. Note the building labeled "Taberna Meritoria" just under the figure of the Virgin in the Nativity scene, with a stream of oil flowing from it; it recalls the legend that a fountain of oil appeared on this spot, prophesying the birth of Christ. Off the piazza's northern side is a street called Via delle Fonte dell'Olio in honor of this miracle. ✉ *Piazza Santa Maria in Trastevere, Trastevere* ☎ *06/5814802* ⊕ *www.santamariaintrastevere.it.*

Terme di Caracalla (*Baths of Caracalla*)
RUINS | FAMILY | The Terme di Caracalla are some of Rome's most massive—yet least visited—ruins. Begun in AD 206 by the emperor Septimius Severus and completed by his son, Caracalla, the 28-acre complex could accommodate 1,600 bathers at a time. Along with an Olympic-size swimming pool and baths, the complex also had two gyms, a library, and gardens. The impressive baths depended on slave labor, particularly the unseen stokers who toiled in subterranean rooms to keep the fires roaring in order to heat the water.

Rather than a simple dip in a tub, Romans turned "bathing" into one of the most lavish leisure activities imaginable. A bath began in the sudatoria, a series of small rooms resembling saunas, which then led to the caldarium, a circular room that was humid rather than simply hot. Here a strigil, or scraper, was used to get the dirt off the skin. Next stop: the warm(-ish) tepidarium, which helped start the cool-down process. Finally, it ended with a splash around the frigidarium, a chilly swimming pool.

Although some black-and-white mosaic fragments remain, most of the opulent mosaics, frescoes, and sculptures have found their way into Rome's museums. Nevertheless, the towering walls and sheer size of the ruins give one of the best glimpses into ancient Rome's ambitions. A new portable video guide allows a glimpse of the past grandeur, with images and audio that describes how the ruins appeared centuries ago. If you're here in summer, don't miss the chance to catch an open-air opera or ballet in the baths, put on by the Teatro dell'Opera di Roma. ✉ *Viale delle Terme di Caracalla, 52, Aventino* ☎ *06/39967702* ⊕ *www.coopculture.it* 💶 *€8 (includes Villa dei Quintili and Tomba di Cecilia Metella); €17 includes video guide* ⊗ *Closed Mon.* Ⓜ *Circo Massimo.*

★ Villa Farnesina
CASTLE/PALACE | Money was no object to the extravagant Agostino Chigi, a banker from Siena who financed many papal projects. His munificence is evident in this elegant villa, built for him in about 1511. Agostino entertained the popes and princes of 16th-century Rome, impressing his guests at riverside suppers by having his servants clear the table by casting the precious silver and gold dinnerware into the Tiber (indeed, nets were unfurled a foot or two beneath the water's surface to retrieve the valuable ware).

In the magnificent Loggia of Psyche on the ground floor, Giulio Romano and others created the frescoes from Raphael's designs.

Raphael's lovely *Galatea* is in the adjacent room. On the floor above you can see the trompe-l'oeil effects in the aptly named Hall of Perspectives by Peruzzi. Agostino Chigi's bedroom, next door, was frescoed by Il Sodoma with the *Wedding of Alexander and Roxanne*, which is considered to be the artist's best work. The palace also houses the Gabinetto Nazionale delle Stampe, a treasure trove of old prints and drawings. ✉ *Via della Lungara, 230, Trastevere* ☎ *06/68027268* ⊕ *www.villafarnesina.it* 🎫 *€12* 🕐 *Closed Sun.*

🍴 Restaurants

Checchino dal 1887

$$$ | **ROMAN** | Literally carved into the side of a hill made up of ancient shards of amphorae, this upscale, family-run establishment has an exceptional wine cellar and stellar contemporary cocktails that incorporate traditional local ingredients. One of the first restaurants to open near Testaccio's (now long-closed) slaughterhouse, it still serves classic offal dishes—though the white-jacketed waiters are happy to suggest other options. **Known for:** old-school Roman cooking; old-school Roman waiters; coda alla vaccinara (Roman-style oxtail). 💲 *Average main: €25* ✉ *Via di Monte Testaccio, 30, Testaccio* ☎ *06/5743816* ⊕ *www.checchino-dal-1887.com* 🕐 *Closed Mon. and Tues., Aug., and 2 wks in Jan.* Ⓜ *Piramide.*

★ Da Enzo al 29

$ | **ROMAN** | In the quieter part of Trastevere, the family-run Da Enzo is everything you would imagine a classic Roman trattoria to be. There are just a few tables, but diners from around the world line up to eat here—a testament to the quality of the food. **Known for:** cacio e pepe (pasta with pecorino-cheese sauce and black pepper), carbonara, and other Roman classics; boisterous, authentic atmosphere; small space with long waits. 💲 *Average main: €14* ✉ *Via dei Vascellari, 29, Trastevere* ☎ *06/5812260* ⊕ *www.daenzoal29.com* 🕐 *Closed Sun. and 2 wks in Aug.*

★ Glass Hostaria

$$$$ | **MODERN ITALIAN** | After 14 years in Austin, Texas, chef Cristina Bowerman returned to Rome to reconnect with her Italian roots, and her cooking is as innovative as the building she works in (Glass has received numerous recognitions for its design as well as its expertly executed cuisine). The menu, which changes frequently, features dishes like a standout steak tartare and lobster polenta with yuba. **Known for:** vegetarian tasting menu; plates inspired by Italy from north to south; more than 600 types of wine. 💲 *Average main: €40* ✉ *Vicolo del 'Cinque, 58, Trastevere* ☎ *06/58335903* ⊕ *www.glasshostaria.it* 🕐 *Closed Mon., Tues., and 2 wks in July. No lunch Wed.–Fri.*

La Gatta Mangiona

$$ | **PIZZA** | **FAMILY** | The pizza at this neighborhood spot is Roman-style—with a thin crust, charred on the edges. All the standard toppings are available, from margherita to buffalo mozzarella and prosciutto, but try one of the newfangled combinations like ricotta and pancetta and edible wildflowers. **Known for:** Thai pizza with tomato sauce, cheese, and spices; pizza-and-wine pairings; great craft beer selection. ⓢ *Average main: €15* ⊠ *Via Federico Ozanam, 30–32, Rome* ☎ *06/65346702* ⊕ *www.lagattamangiona.com* ⊗ *No lunch.*

★ Marigold

$ | **SCANDINAVIAN** | Run by a Danish-Italian duo, this hip restaurant has a Scandinavian-meets-Roman design and menu. It draws a young, international crowd who come for the sourdough, cinnamon buns, and veggie-forward dishes. **Known for:** sourdough breads and other baked goods; specialty coffee; minimalist Italian design. ⓢ *Average main: €13* ⊠ *Via Giovanni da Empoli, 37, Testaccio* ☎ *06/87725679* ⊕ *marigoldroma.com* ⊗ *Closed Mon. and Tues., 3 wks in Aug., and 2 wks in Dec. No dinner* Ⓜ *Ostiense.*

★ Mordi e Vai

$ | **ITALIAN** | **FAMILY** | This family-run stall at what will forever be called the "New" Testaccio Market (it moved in 2012) sells the best sandwiches in town. Meatballs, tongue, tripe, and other Roman classics are generously smothered on fresh bread, and there is always a vegetarian option, too. **Known for:** alesso (slow-cooked beef) sandwiches; breaded meatballs; long lines at lunchtime. ⓢ *Average main: €5* ⊠ *Testaccio Market, Box 15, Via Beniamino Franklin, Rome* ☎ *347/6632731* ⊕ *www.facebook.com/mordievai* ⊗ *Closed Sun. No dinner.*

Pizzeria Ai Marmi

$ | **PIZZA** | **FAMILY** | This place is packed pretty much every night with diners munching on crisp pizzas that come out of the wood-burning ovens at top speed. It's best not to go during peak dining hours, so go early or late if you don't want to wait. **Known for:** excellent wood-oven pizzas; fried starters such as supplì (breaded fried rice balls); open until midnight for a late-night bite. ⓢ *Average main: €13* ⊠ *Viale Trastevere, 53, Trastevere* ☎ *06/5800919* ⊕ *www.facebook.com/aimarmi* ⊗ *Closed Wed. and 3 wks in Aug. No lunch.*

☕ Coffee and Quick Bites

★ Biscottificio Innocenti

$ | **ITALIAN** | **FAMILY** | The scent of cookies wafts out into the street as you approach this family-run bakery, where a small team makes sweet treats the old-school way in a massive oven bought in the 1960s. There are dozens of varieties of baked goods, mostly sweet but some savory. **Known for:** old-school family-run bakery; dozens of varieties of baked goods; brutti ma buoni ("ugly but good") hazelnut cookies. ⑤ *Average main: €3* ✉ *Via della Luce, 21, Trastevere* ☎ *06/5803926* ⊕ *www.facebook.com/BiscottificioInnocenti* ⊙ *Closed Sun. and 2 wks in Aug.*

Otaleg!

$ | ICE CREAM | FAMILY | A slow wander through town for a scoop of gelato after lunch or dinner is a summer sport in Rome. Galley-sized Otaleg is a must in Trastevere, where gelato master Marco Radicioni dreams up concoctions like *croccante totale* (completely crunchy) with fiordilatte, toasted nuts, sesame, and honey, as well as perfectly distilled seasonal fruit sorbets made with produce from the nearby open-air market in Piazza San Cosimato. **Known for:** high-quality ingredients; creative flavors; neighborhood go-to. ⑤ *Average main: €5* ✉ *Via di San Cosimato, 14a, Trastevere* ☎ *338/6515450* ⊕ *www.otaleg.com.*

Suppli Roma

$ | ROMAN | FAMILY | Trastevere's best supplì (Roman-style rice croquettes) have been served at this hole-in-the-wall takeout spot since 1979. At lunchtime, the line spills out onto the street with locals who've come for the namesake treats, as well as fried baccalà fillets and stuffed zucchini flowers. **Known for:** old-fashioned baked pizza with spicy marinara sauce; gnocchi on Thursday (the traditional day for it in Rome); classic fried risotto ball with ragù or cacio e pepe. ⑤ *Average main: €6* ✉ *Via di San Francesco a Ripa, 137, Trastevere* ☎ *06/5897110* ⊕ *www.suppliroma.it* ⊙ *Closed Sun. and 2 wks in Aug.*

Hotels

Casa di Santa Francesca Romana a Ponte Rotto

$$ | HOTEL | In the heart of Trastevere but tucked away from the hustle and bustle of the medieval quarter, this comfortable, affordable hotel in a former monastery is centered on a lovely green courtyard and still has a chapel off the corridor. **Pros:** rates can't be beat; triple rooms for small groups; free breakfast. **Cons:** a bit far from Metro, but there are tram and bus stops nearby; few amenities besides TV room and reading room; main door locks at midnight, requiring guests to ring the bell. ⑤ *Rooms from: €140* ✉ *Via dei Vascellari, 61, Trastevere* ☎ *06/5812125* ⊕ *www.sfromana.it* ⇨ *37 rooms* ⓘ◎ǀ *Free Breakfast.*

Did You Know?

From Gianicolo (Janiculum Hill), the views of the tightly knit, bohemian Trastevere neighborhood and Isola Tiberina (Tiber Island) are particularly enchanting at dusk.

Hotel Carmel

$$ | **HOTEL** | In the heart of Trastevere and across the Tiber from the main synagogue in the Jewish Ghetto is Rome's only kosher hotel, a friendly and budget-friendly place to stay. **Pros:** lovely dining terrace outside; kosher breakfast can be arranged for €5 extra per person per day; check-in starts at noon. **Cons:** no frills; air-conditioning is a bit weak; some rooms share a bath. $ *Rooms from: €130* ✉ *Via Goffredo Mameli, 11, Trastevere* ☎ *06/5809921* ⊕ *www.hotelcarmel.it* ⇌ *11 rooms* ⊚ *Free Breakfast.*

Hotel San Anselmo

$$$ | **HOTEL** | Set in a *molto* charming garden atop the Aventine Hill, this refurbished 19th-century villa is a romantic retreat. **Pros:** free Wi-Fi; historic building with artful interior; garden where you can enjoy breakfast. **Cons:** some rooms are quite small; limited public transportation; no full restaurant. $ *Rooms from: €220* ✉ *Piazza San Anselmo, 2, Aventino* ☎ *06/570057* ⊕ *www.aventinohotels.com/sananselmo* ⇌ *34 rooms* ⊚ *Free Breakfast* Ⓜ *Circo Massimo.*

Hotel Santa Maria

$$$ | **HOTEL** | A Trastevere treasure with a pedigree going back four centuries, this ivy-covered, mansard-roofed, rosy-brick-red, erstwhile Renaissance-era convent—just steps away from the glorious Santa Maria in Trastevere church and a few blocks from the Tiber—has sweet and simple guest rooms: a mix of brick walls, "cotto" tile floors, oak furniture, and matching bedspreads and curtains. **Pros:** a quaint and pretty oasis in a central location; spacious rooms for groups; lovely rooftop terrace with views across the city. **Cons:** tricky to find; not the best value for money; church bells may wake light sleepers. $ *Rooms from: €250* ✉ *Vicolo del Piede, 2, Trastevere* ☎ *06/5894626* ⊕ *www.hotelsantamariatrastevere.it* ⇌ *20 rooms* ⊚ *Free Breakfast.*

Hotel Trastevere

$$ | **HOTEL** | This hotel captures the villagelike charm of the Trastevere district and offers basic, clean, comfortable rooms. **Pros:** good rates for location; convenient to tram and bus; friendly staff. **Cons:** rooms are a little worn around the edges; few amenities; standard rooms are quite small. $ *Rooms from: €180* ✉ *Via Luciano Manara, 24/a, Trastevere* ☎ *06/5814713* ⊕ *www.hoteltrastevere.net* ⇌ *14 rooms* ⊚ *Free Breakfast.*

Relais Le Clarisse

$$ | **B&B/INN** | Set within the former cloister grounds of the Santa Chiara order, with beautiful gardens, Le Clarisse makes you feel like a personal guest at a friend's villa, thanks to the comfortable size of the guest rooms and personalized service. **Pros:** spacious rooms with comfy beds; high-tech showers/tubs with good water pressure; complimentary high-speed Wi-Fi. **Cons:** this part of Trastevere can be noisy at night; check when booking as you may be put in neighboring building; no restaurant or bar. ⑤ *Rooms from: €200* ✉ *Via Cardinale Merry del Val, 20, Trastevere* ☎ *06/58334437* ⊕ *www.leclarissetrastevere.com* ⇨ *17 rooms* ⑩ *Free Breakfast.*

Nightlife

★ Freni e Frizioni
COCKTAIL BARS | This hipster hangout is great for a sunset aperitivo or for late-night socializing. Though the vibe is artsy and laid-back, the bartenders take their cocktails seriously—and have the awards to prove it. In warmer weather, the crowd overflows into the large terrazza overlooking the Tiber and the side streets of Trastevere. ✉ *Via del Politeama, 4, Trastevere* ☎ *06/45497499* ⊕ *www.freniefrizioni.com.*

Ma Che Siete Venuti a Fa
PUB | Affectionately shortened to "Makke" by Romans, this tiny pub can't contain the number of beer lovers who flock here at all hours to indulge in a craft pint, or three. Patrons spill out onto the sidewalk behind Piazza Trilussa, sipping the carefully selected artisan brews that arrive from around the world. There is a rotating selection on the 16 taps, and an impressive list of bottled beer. ✉ *Via Benedetta, 25, Trastevere* ☎ *06/42918213* ⊕ *football-pub.com.*

Rivendita
WINE BAR | The full name is "Rivendita: Libri Teatro e Cioccolata" and that's exactly what you'll find in this charming hole-in-the-wall: books and chocolate. Open only in the evenings, the used-bookstore-bar combo offers wine, sweet cocktails, or coffee served in shot glass–sized cups of pure chocolate. ✉ *Vicolo del Cinque, 11/a, Trastevere* ☎ *06/58301868.*

★ Tram Depot
COCKTAIL BARS | A coffee stand by day and cocktail bar by night, this outdoor establishment began life as a city tram car back in 1903. Now the historic carriage has been converted to a kiosk permanently stationed on a park corner with retro tables and garden seating. A trendy crowd descends at sunset for an evening spritz, and seats are at a premium until the wee hours of the morning. Since it is entirely outside, Tram Depot is mainly open in the warmer months of the year (April through November); but weather permitting, the kiosk stays open on the weekends year-round. ✉ *Via Marmorata, 13, Testaccio* ☎ *380/6455154* ⊕ *www.facebook.com/TramDepotOfficial* Ⓜ *Piramide.*

Index

A

Addresses, *32*
Air travel, *34–36*
Albergo Santa Chiara 🏨, *117*
Aleph Rome Hotel, Curio Collection by Hilton 🏨, *137*
Altar of Augustan Peace, *129, 132*
Altar of the Nation, *132*
Anantara Palazzo Naiadi Rome Hotel 🏨, *162*
Ancient Rome
  coffee and quick bites, 77
  hotels, 79–80
  restaurants, 74, 76–77
  sights, 60–63, 66–67, 70–74
  time management, 64
  top experiences, 64
  tours, 60–63
  transportation, 64
Anima ✕, *160*
Antica Enoteca, *143*
Antico Albergo del Sole al Pantheon 🏨, *118*
Antico Caffè Greco ✕, *136*
Arch of Constantine, *60*
Arch of Septimius Severus, *63, 66*
Architecture, *16*
Armando al Pantheon ✕, *114*
Art academies, *160*
Arts festivals, *53*
Aventino, *46, 173, 176–177, 178, 179, 184*

B

Babuino *181* 🏨, *137, 140*
Baccano ✕, *136*
Ba'Ghetto ✕, *114–115*
Baglioni Hotel Regina 🏨, *140*
Bakeries, *117, 160–161*
Bars and lounges
  Campo de' Fiori, 115–116, 121
  Piazza di Spagna, 143
  Piazza Navona, 120–121
  Trastevere, 185
  Villa Borghese, 165–166
Baths of Caracalla, *179*
Bicycling, *16*
Biscottificio Innocenti ✕, *181–182*
Bonci Pizzarium ✕, *94*
Books, *28–30*
Borgo, *46, 85, 87, 94, 95, 96*
Bridges, *91, 94*
Bus travel, *36–37, 40–41*

C

Cafés, *117, 136–137*
Caffè Canova-Tadolini ✕, *136–137*
Campo de' Fiori
  hotels, 118, 119–120
  nightlife, 121
  restaurants, 115–116
  shopping, 121–122
  sights, 110–111, 113–114
  top experiences, 104
  tours, 100–103
Campo Marzio, *105*
Canova ✕, *160*
Capitoline Hill, *57, 62, 65*
Capo d'Africa 🏨, *79*
Car travel and rentals, *37–39*
Cartoleria Pantheon dal 1910, *121*
Casa di Santa Francesca Romana a Ponte Rotto 🏨, *182*
Castel Sant'Angelo, *90*
Castles and palaces, *90, 106–107, 132–133, 179–180*
Centrale Montemartini, *23, 176*
Checchino dal 1887 ✕, *180*
Chez Dede, *121–122*
Chorus Café ✕, *94*
Churches, *32–33*
  Ancient Rome, 72–74
  Aventino, 178
  Campo de' Fiori, 113
  Piazza Navona, 102, 112–113
  Trastevere, 178–179
  Trevi, 134
  Vatican, 88–89
  Villa Borghese, 159
Circus Maximus, *67, 70*
Clothing stores, *21, 121–122, 144, 166*
Coffee and quick bites, *77, 116, 117, 180–182*
Colosseum, *60, 66, 70–71*
Columns, *63, 70*
Contrario Vineria con Cucina ✕, *74*
Cuisine, *18–19*

D

Da Enzo al *29* ✕, *180*
Dagnino ✕, *160–161*
Del Frate ✕, *94*
Department stores, *144*
Dining, *16, 43–45.* ⇨ *See also Restaurants*
D.O.M Hotel Roma 🏨, *118*
Dress codes, *32–33*

E

E-bikes, *16*
Easter, *24*
Emma Pizzeria ✕, *115*
Enoteca al Parlamento Achilli, *120–121*
Enoteca La Torre Villa Laetitia ✕, *94–95*
Equilibrio, *51*
Esedra *58, 166*
Esquilino, *46*
Estate Romana, *52*
Etiquette, *33*
Ex Libris, *143*

F

Fall travel, *26*
Fatamorgana Monti ✕, *77*
Ferragosto, *25, 33*

Festa del Cinema di Roma, *53*
Festa della Repubblica, *25*
Festivals and events, *24, 25, 51–53*
Field of Mars, *105*
First Arte, The 🛏 , *162*
Fontana del Mascherone, *114*
Fountains, *105, 106, 128, 135–136, 159*
Four Fountains, *159*
French Academy of Rome, The, *160*
Freni e Frizioni, *185*

G

G-Rough Hotel 🛏 , *118*
Galleria Alberto Sordi, *144*
Galleria Borghese, *22, 146, 151–153*
Galleria Nazionale d'Arte Antica, *156–157*
Gardens, *177–178*
Gelateria Del Teatro ✕ , *116*
Giolitti ✕ , *116*
Glass Hostaria ✕ , *180*
Gran Priorato di Roma dell'Ordine di Malta, *176–177*
Green Market Festival, *51*

H

Hassler, The 🛏 , *140*
Health, *48*
Historic homes, *160*
Holy Mary of Prayer and Death, *114*
Hotel Abruzzi 🛏 , *118*
Hotel Atlante Star 🛏 , *96*
Hotel Campo de' Fiori 🛏 , *119*
Hotel Carmel 🛏 , *184*
Hotel Chapter Roma 🛏 , *119*
Hotel Condotti 🛏 , *140*
Hotel de la Ville 🛏 , *140–141*

Hotel de' Ricci 🛏 , *119–120*
Hotel de Russie 🛏 , *162, 164*
Hotel dei Mellini 🛏 , *96*
Hotel Eden 🛏 , *141*
Hotel Julia 🛏 , *141–142*
Hotel Lancelot 🛏 , *79*
Hotel Locarno 🛏 , *164*
Hotel Ponte Sisto 🛏 , *120*
Hotel San Anselmo 🛏 , *184*
Hotel Santa Maria 🛏 , *184*
Hotel Sant'Anna Roma 🛏 , *96*
Hotel Trastevere 🛏 , *184*
Hotel Vilòn 🛏 , *142*
Hotels, *17, 45–47*
Ancient Rome, *79–80*
Aventino, *184*
Campo de' Fiori, *118, 119–120*
Jewish Ghetto, *119*
Piazza di Spagna, *137, 140–141, 142*
Piazza Navona, *117–118, 120*
Repubblica, *162, 165*
Trastevere, *182, 184–185*
Trevi, *141–142*
Vatican, *96, 98*
Villa Borghese, *162, 164–165*
House of Augustus, *66–67*
Hoxton, Rome, The 🛏 , *164*

I

I Concerti nel Parco, *52*
Ice cream shops, *77, 116, 182*
Il Bocconcino ✕ , *76*
Il Goccetto, *121*
Il Marchese, *143*
Il Marmoraro, *166*
Il Palazzetto Wine Bar, *143*
Il Sanlorenzo ✕ , *115*
Il Tempietto, *51*
Il Tempio di Iside ✕ , *76*
Imàgo ✕ , *137*

INEO ✕ , *161*
Islands, *177*
Italian language, *54–55*
Itineraries, *56–58*

J

Jerry Thomas Speakeasy, *121*
Jewish Ghetto
coffee and quick bites, *117*
hotels, *119*
restaurants, *114–115, 117*
sights, *106, 111–112, 113*
tours, *100–103*
transportation, *104*
J.K. Place Roma 🛏 , *142*

K

Knights of Malta priory, *176–177*

L

La Gatta Mangiona ✕ , *181*
La Matriciana dal 1870 ✕ , *161*
La Pergola ✕ , *161*
La Rinascente, *144*
La Taverna dei Fori Imperiali ✕ , *76*
La Zanzara ✕ , *95*
L'Archivio di Monserrato, *122*
Laura Urbinati, *166*
LGBTQ+, *49, 52, 98*
Lodging, *45–47.* ⇨ *See also Hotels*

M

Ma Che Siete Venuti a Fa, *185*
Maalot Roma 🛏 , *142*
MACRO (Museo de Arte Contemporáneo de Roma), *22, 153*
Maison Halaby, *122*
Mama Shelter Roma 🛏 , *98*
Marigold ✕ , *181*
Markets, *106, 110–111, 171*

Massimo Maria Melis, *122*
Mausoleum of Augustus, *127, 129*
MAXXI (Museo Nazionale delle Arti del XXI Secolo), *23, 153, 156*
Mercato Campagna Amica, *106*
Metro, *41–42*
Metropolita, *165–166*
Moma ✕ , *137*
Monte Mario, *46, 161, 165*
Monteverde, *172, 173*
Monuments, *129, 132*
Mordi e Vai ✕ , *181*
Movies, *28–30*
Musei Capitolini, *32, 71–72*
Museums, *22–23*
  Ancient Rome, *32, 71–72*
  Testaccio, *176*
  Vatican, *22, 82–85, 90–91*
  Villa Borghese, *22, 23, 146, 151–153, 156–157*
Music festivals, *51, 52, 53*

N

Natale Festival, *53*
National Etruscan Museum, *22, 156*
National Gallery of Modern Art, *23, 153*
National Museum of 21st Century (MAXXI), *23, 153, 156*
Nerva Boutique Hotel 🏨 , *79*
New Prison, *114*
NH Collection Roma Fori Imperiali 🏨 , *79*
Nightlife
  Campo de' Fiori, *121*
  Piazza di Spagna, *143*
  Piazza Navona, *120–121*
  Testaccio, *1854*
  Trastevere, *185*
  Villa Borghese, *165–166*
9 Hotel Cesàri 🏨 , *120*

O

Otaleg! ✕ , *182*

P

Palatine Hill, *62, 63, 64, 66, 67*
Palazzo Altemps, *106–107*
Palazzo Barberini, *156–157*
Palazzo Colonna, *132–133*
Palazzo Dama Hotel 🏨 , *164*
Palazzo Doria Pamphilj, *22, 133*
Palazzo Falconieri, *114*
Palazzo Farnese, *114*
Palazzo Manfredi 🏨 , *80*
Palazzo Massimo alle Terme, *157*
Palazzo Sacchetti, *113–114*
Palazzo Velabro 🏨 , *80*
Pantheon, *100, 107, 110*
Pantheon Iconic Rome Hotel, Autograph Collection, The 🏨 , *120*
Parco dei Principi Grand Hotel & Spa 🏨 , *164*
Parioli, *46, 146, 164*
Parking, *38*
Passports, *48*
Pasticceria Boccione ✕ , *117*
Piazza Augusto Imperatore, *126–127*
Piazza Campo de' Fiori, *103, 110–111*
Piazza del Popolo, *46, 134, 148, 158*
Piazza del Quirinale, *158*
Piazza della Repubblica, *157–158*
Piazza di San Francesco d'Assisi, *170*
Piazza di Santa Maria in Trastevere, *170, 177*
Piazza di Spagna
  hotels, *137, 140–141, 142*
  nightlife, *143*
  restaurants, *136–137*
  sights, *129, 132, 135*
  top experiences, *128*
  tours, *124–127*
  transportation, *128*
Piazza Navona
  coffee and quick bites, *116, 117*
  hotels, *117–118, 120*
  nightlife, *120–121*
  restaurants, *114, 116, 117*
  shopping, *121, 122*
  sights, *106–107, 110, 111, 112–113*
  top experiences, *104*
  tours, *100–103*
  transportation, *104*
Piazza San Pietro, *91*
Piazza Trilussa, *168, 170*
Piazza Venezia, *134*
Pierluigi ✕ , *115*
Pincio Promenade, *158–159*
Pineider, *144*
Pizzeria Ai Marmi ✕ , *181*
Plazas and squares
  Campo de' Fiori, *103, 113–114*
  Piazza Augusto Imperatore, *126–127*
  Piazza Navona, *111*
  Trastevere, *168, 170, 177*
  Trevi, *134*
  Vatican, *91*
  Villa Borghese, *46, 148, 157–158*
Ponte Sant'Angelo, *91, 94*
Portico d'Ottavia, *111–112*
Prati, *46, 53, 87, 90, 94–96, 98*
Pride Week, *52*
Promenades, *158–159*
Public transportation, *32, 39–42*

R

Relais Le Clarisse 🏨 , *184–185*
Repubblica
  hotels, *162, 165*
  restaurants, *160–161*
  shopping, *166*
  sights, *22, 153, 157–158, 159*
  transportation, *150*
Restaurants, *16, 32, 43–45*
  Ancient Rome, *74, 76–77*

Campo de' Fiori, 115–116
Jewish Ghetto, 114–115, 117
Piazza di Spagna, 136–137
Piazza Navona, 114, 116, 117
Repubblica, 160–161
Testaccio, 180, 181
Trastevere, 180–182
Trevi, 136
Vatican, 94–96
Villa Borghese, 160–162

Ristorante All'Oro ✕, *162*

Ristorante Arlù ✕, *95*

Rivendita, *185*

Rocco Ristorante, *76–77*

Roma Pass, *32*

Roma Summer Fest, *52*

RomaEuropa, *53*

Roman Forum, *60–63*

Rome Cavalieri, A Waldorf Astoria Hotel 🏨, *165*

Rome EDITION, The 🏨, *165*

Roscioli Salumeria con Cucina ✕, *115–116*

Roseto Comunale, *177–178*

Ruins, *66–67, 70–71, 74, 111–112, 179*

S

Safety, *49*
San Eligio, *113*
San Luigi dei Francesi, *112*
San Pietro in Vincoli, *72–73*
Santa Maria della Pace, *112–113*
Santa Maria della Vittoria, *159*
Santa Maria in Cosmedin, *178*
Santa Maria in Trastevere, *178–179*
Santa Maria Maggiore, *73–74*
Sant'Eustachio il Caffè ✕, *117*
Sant'Ignazio, *134*
Schostal, *144*
Shopping, *20–21, 49*

Campo de' Fiori, 121–122
Piazza Navona, 121, 122
Repubblica, 166
Testaccio, 171
Trevi, 143
Villa Borghese, 166

Sinagoga, *113*

Sistine Chapel, *85, 89*

Sorpasso ✕, *95–96*

Spanish Steps, The, *126, 135*

Spring FAI Days, *51*

Spring travel, *25*

St. Peter's Basilica, *32–33, 88–89*

St. Regis Rome, The 🏨, *165*

Stravinskij Bar at the Hotel de Russie, *166*

Streets, *113–114, 134*

Subway system, *41–42*

Summer travel, *26*

Superga, *144*

Suppli Roma ✕, *182*

Synagogues, *113*

T

Taxes, *32, 49*
Tazza d'Oro ✕, *117*
Television, *28, 30*
Temple of Castor and Pollux, *62*
Temple of Venus, *62*
Temples, *62, 107, 110*
Testaccio
nightlife, *1854*
restaurants, *180, 181*
shopping, *171*
sights, *176*
tours, *168–171*
transportation, *172*

Testaccio Market, *171*
Tiber Island, *177*
Tipping, *50*
Tombs, *127, 129*
Tourist City Tax, *32*
Tours
Ancient Rome, *60–63*
Campo de' Fiori, *100–103*
Jewish Ghetto, *100–103*
Piazza di Spagna, *124–127*
Piazza Navona, *100–103*
Testaccio, *168–171*
Trastevere, *168–171*
Trevi, *124–127*

Vatican, 82–85
Villa Borghese, 146–149

Train travel, *42*

Trajan's Column, *63, 70*

Tram Depot, *185*

Trams, *40–41*

Transportation, *16, 32, 34–42*
Ancient Rome, *64*
Campo de' Fiori, *104*
Jewish Ghetto, *104*
Piazza di Spagna, *128*
Piazza Navona, *104*
Repubblica, *150*
Testaccio, *172*
Trastevere, *172*
Trevi, *128*
Vatican, *86*
Villa Borghese, *150*

Trastevere
coffee and quick bites, *180–182*
hotels, *182, 184–185*
neighborhood descriptions, *46, 173*
nightlife, *185*
restaurants, *180–182*
sights, *168, 170, 177, 178–180*
top reasons to go, *172*
tours, *168–171*
transportation, *172*

Travel seasons, *24–27, 33*

Trevi
hotels, *141–142*
neighborhood descriptions, *129*
restaurants, *136*
shopping, *143*
sights, *132–134, 135–136*
top experiences, *128*
tours, *124–127*
transportation, *128*

Trevi Fountain, *128, 135–136*

Turtle Fountain, *105, 106*

V

Vacation seasons, *33*
Vatican, The
hotels, *96, 98*
restaurants, *94–96*
sights, *82–85, 88–91, 94*
time management, *86*
top experiences, *86*
tours, *82–85*
transportation, *86*

Vatican Museums, 22, 82–85, 90–91
Via del Corso, 134
Via Giulia, 113–114
Via Sacra, 62, 74
Victor Emmanuel II Monument, 132
Viewpoints, 158–159
Villa Ada Festival, 52
Villa Borghese
  hotels, 162, 164–165
  nightlife, 165–166
  restaurants, 160–162
  shopping, 166
  sights, 151–153, 156–160
top experiences, 150
tours, 146–149
transportation, 150
Villa Farnesina, 168, 179–180
Villa Medici, 160
Visas, 48
Vitala Festival, 53
ViVi Piazza Venezia , 77

W

W Rome , 142
Walking tours
  Pizza Navona, Campo de' Fiori, and Jewish Ghetto, 100–103
  Roman Forum, 60–63
  Trastevere and Testaccio, 168–171
  Trevi and Piazza di Spagna, 124–127
  Villa Borghese, 146–149
Winter travel, 27

Z

Zia Rosetta ✕, 77

Photo Credits

Front Cover: Alan Smithers/Alamy Stock Photo[Descr.: Trevi Fountain in Rome, Italy.]
Back cover, from left to right: Nicola Forenza/iStockphoto. RudyBalasko/iStockphoto. Xantana/iStockphoto. **Spine:** Gennaro Leonardi/iStockphoto. **Interior, from left to right:** Rudy Sulgan/GettyImages (1). Johnypan/Dreamstime (2). **Chapter 1: Experience Rome:** SJ Travel Photo and Video/Shutterstock (6-7). F11photo/Shutterstock (8-9). Marcomerry/Shutterstock (9). Muharremz/Shutterstock (9). Catarina Belova/Shutterstock (10). Sonse/Wikimedia (10). S.Borisov/Shutterstock (11). Alexander Prokopenko/Shutterstock (12). Stefano Valeri/Dreamstime (12). Nido Huebl/Shutterstock (12). Gnoparus/Shutterstock (13). Beats1/Shutterstock (18). Mavo/Shutterstock (19). Lucian Milasan/Shutterstock (20). Elena Pominova/Shutterstock (20). Andriy Blokhin/Shutterstock (20). Uly Prokopiv/Shutterstock (20). Cavan-Images/Shutterstock (21). Christian Creixell/Alamy Stock Photo (22). Isogood_patrick/Shutterstock (22). Wjarek/Shutterstock (22). Valery Rokhin/Shutterstock (22). SimoneN/Shutterstock (23). Xbrchx/iStockphoto (24). Kinoalyse/Dreamstime (25). Cris Foto/Shutterstock (26). Essevu/Shutterstock (27). **Chapter 3: Ancient Rome:** Leoks/Shutterstock (59). Anamejia18/Dreamstime (62). Misterlvad/Shutterstock (63). Paul D'Innocenzo (67). Preto_perola/iStockphoto (75). Sandro Pavlov/Shutterstock (78). **Chapter 4: The Vatican:** Banauke/Shutterstock (81). Izzet Keribar/GettyImages (84). Andres Solaro/GettyImages (85). Vladimir Sazonov/Shutterstock (95). Blue Planet Studio/Shutterstock (97). **Chapter 5: Piazza Navona, Campo de' Fiori, and the Jewish Ghetto:** Nikada/iStockphoto (99). Diego Fiore/iStockphoto (102). Francesco Riccardo Iacomino/GettyImages (103). Realy Easy Star/Alamy Stock Photo (107). Adam eastland /Alamy Stock Photo (116). Ale Argentieri/Shutterstock (119). **Chapter 6: Trevi and Piazza di Spagna:** Belenos/ Shutterstock (123). Tunart/GettyImages (126). Nekomura/Shutterstock (127). Suchart Boonyavech/Shutterstock (138-139). Sara Corso/Shutterstock (141). **Chapter 7: Villa Borghese and Environs:** Catarina Belova/Shutterstock (145). Vololibero/GettyImages (148). Vololibero/Shutterstock (149). Public Domain (152). Adam eastland/Alamy Stock Photo (163). **Chapter 8: Trastevere, Testaccio, and Environs:** Catarina Belova/Shutterstock (167). Catarina Belova/Shutterstock (170). Sergey-73/Shutterstock (171). Essevu/Shutterstock (183). **About Our Writers:** All photos are courtesy of the writers except for the following.

Every effort has been made to trace the copyright holders, and we apologize in advance for any accidental errors. We would be happy to apply the corrections in the following edition of this publication.

Fodor's Pocket Guides ROME

Publisher: Stephen Horowitz, *General Manager*

Editorial: Douglas Stallings, *Editorial Director;* Jill Fergus, Amanda Sadlowski, *Senior Editors;* Brian Eschrich, Alexis Kelly, *Editors;* Angelique Kennedy-Chavannes, Yoojin Shin, *Associate Editors*

Design: Tina Malaney, *Director of Design and Production;* Jessica Gonzalez, *Senior Designer;* Jaimee Shaye, *Graphic Design Associate*

Production: Jennifer DePrima, *Editorial Production Manager;* Elyse Rozelle, *Senior Production Editor;* Monica White, *Production Editor*

Maps: Rebecca Baer, *Map Director;* Mark Stroud (Moon Street Cartography), *Cartographer*

Photography: Viviane Teles, *Director of Photography;* Neha Gupta, Payal Gupta, Ashok Kumar, *Photo Editors;* Jade Rodgers, Shanelle Jacobs, *Photo Production Intern*

Business and Operations: Chuck Hoover, *Chief Marketing Officer;* Robert Ames, *Group General Manager*

Public Relations and Marketing: Joe Ewaskiw, *Senior Director of Communications and Public Relations*

Fodors.com: Jeremy Tarr, *Editorial Director;* Rachael Levitt, *Managing Editor*

Technology: Jon Atkinson, *Executive Director of Technology;* Rudresh Teotia, *Associate Director of Technology;* Alison Lieu, *Project Manager*

Writer: Laura Itzkowitz
Editor: Yoojin Shin
Production Editor: Jennifer DePrima

Copyright © 2025 by Fodor's Travel, a division of MH Sub I, LLC, dba Internet Brands.

Fodor's is a registered trademark of Internet Brands, Inc. All rights reserved. Published in the United States by Fodor's Travel, a division of Internet Brands, Inc. No maps, illustrations, or other portions of this book may be reproduced in any form without written permission from the publisher.

6th Edition

ISBN 978-1-64097-790-7

ISSN 1094-4001

All details in this book are based on information supplied to us at press time. Always confirm information when it matters, especially if you're making a detour to visit a specific place. Fodor's expressly disclaims any liability, loss, or risk, personal or otherwise, that is incurred as a consequence of the use of any of the contents of this book.

SPECIAL SALES

This book is available at special discounts for bulk purchases for sales promotions or premiums. For more information, e-mail SpecialMarkets@fodors.com.

PRINTED IN CANADA

10 9 8 7 6 5 4 3 2 1

About Our Writers

Laura Itzkowitz is a freelance writer and editor based in Rome with an MFA in creative writing and a passion for covering travel, arts and culture, lifestyle, design, and food and wine. Her writing has appeared in *Travel + Leisure, Architectural Digest, Vogue, Food & Wine, Condé Nast Traveler, AFAR,* and others. Follow her on Instagram and X @lauraitzkowitz, and subscribe to her weekly newsletter at ⊕ *newromantimes.substack.com*. She wrote several new features for this guidebook, including all the walking and museum tours.

In addition, the listings in this book were updated with the help of our Rome guidebook team: **Natalie Kennedy** and **Erica Firpo.**